ff

HIDDEN LIVES, HIDDEN DEATHS

South Africa's Crippling of a Continent

Victoria Brittain

faber and faber
LONDON · BOSTON

First published in 1988
by Faber and Faber Limited
3 Queen Square London WC1N 3AU
This new paperback edition first published in 1990

Typeset by Goodfellow & Egan Ltd, Cambridge
Printed in Great Britain by
Richard Clay Ltd, Bungay, Suffolk
All rights reserved

British Library Cataloguing in Publication Data

Brittain, Victoria
Hidden lives, hidden deaths: South Africa's
crippling of a continent.
1. South Africa——Military policy
1. Title
355′.0335′68   UA856

ISBN 0-571-14216-8

To the memory of Thomas Sankara, who made Burkina Faso a symbol of a different Africa, and who was murdered because his courage, his clarity and his purity were an inspiration to change. And to the memory of Ruth First – assassinated by a South African letter bomb.

Contents

Acknowledgements

So many people, especially in Southern Africa, have helped me with this book and I want to thank them all for their generous time and patience. Some, who know how much I owe them, will prefer not to be named.

I particularly want to thank the Angolan Women's Organization, OMA, its President Ruth Neto, and Basil Davidson, Augusta Conchiglia and Niel Ruiz Guerra for making so many things possible for me.

I also want to thank my colleague Jonathan Steele and my editor Will Sulkin for many comments, great improvements to the first draft, and much encouragement.

List of Maps

Acronyms and Abbreviations

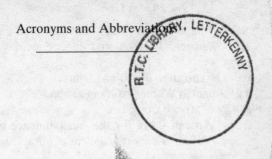

ANC – African National Congress. Leaders: Nelson Mandela and Oliver Tambo. Leading South African opposition movement, banned in South Africa, supported by most African countries, Non-Aligned Movement, Scandinavian countries and all socialist countries.

Derg – Ethiopia's ruling group.

DTA – Democratic Turnhalle Alliance.

EPDA – Ethiopian People's Democratic Alliance.

FAPLA – Popular Armed Forces for the Liberation of Angola, the government army since independence.

FLS – Front-line States: Angola, Botswana, Mozambique, Tanzania, Zambia and Zimbabwe.

FNLA – National Front for the Liberation of Angola. Leader: Holden Roberto. Supported by the CIA, China and Zaïre.

FRELIMO – Front for the Liberation of Mozambique. Leaders: Eduardo Mondlane (assassinated by Portuguese agents), Samora Machel, Joachim Chissano. Formed government at independence.

IMF – International Monetary Fund. Washington-based financial institution set up with the World Bank after the Second World War to harmonize international financial flows and promote economic growth. Its changing role and increasing influence in African politics is a new phenomenon.

ISHR – International Society for Human Rights.

MNR – Mozambique National Resistance, also known as RENAMO. Leader: Alfred Ohaklama. Set up by Rhodesian Special Branch.

MPLA – Popular Movement for the Liberation of Angola. First leader: Dr Agostinho Neto, later, Jose Eduardo Dos

Santos. Supported by Cuba, Soviet Union and other socialist countries. Formed first independent government in 1975.

OAU – Organization of African Unity.

OMA – Angolan Women's Organization.

PAC – Pan-African Congress.

PAIGC – African Party for the Independence of Guinea and Cape Verde. Leader: Amilcar Cabral (assassinated by Portuguese agents).

PIDE – Portuguese secret police, long in co-operation with Jonas Savimbi's UNITA and with Rhodesian Security in setting up MNR.

PLAN – People's Liberation Army of Namibia, military wing of SWAPO.

PNDC – Provisional National Defence Council, ruling group in Ghana under Flight Lieutenant Jerry Rawlings.

Polisario – independence movement of Moroccan-occupied Western Sahara (also known as SADR, see below)

SACC – South African Council of Churches. Secretary-General: Frank Chikane, leading member of the UDF; former Secretary-Generals: Beyer Naude and Desmond Tutu.

SADCC – South African Development Co-ordinating Conference – a nine-country economic grouping set up to reroute economic patterns of Southern Africa away from South Africa.

SADF – South African Defence Force.

SADR – Saharan Arab Democratic Republic (Western Sahara).

SAYCO – South African Youth Congress. Effectively banned 25 February 1988.

SPLA – Sudan People's Liberation Army.

SWAPO – South West African People's Organization.

SWATF – South West African Territorial Force, the army formed by South Africa in Namibia to fight the independence movement SWAPO.

UDF – United Democratic Front, grouping of nearly 1,000 South African organizations including trade unions, churches and community groups who support the ANC's Freedom Charter. Activities banned 25 February 1988.

UNHCR – the United Nations High Commission for Refugees.

UNITA – Union for the Total Liberation of Angola. Leader: Jonas Savimbi. Supported by South Africa and the United States.

USAID – United States Agency for International Development.

ZANU – Zimbabwe African National Union. Sole political party in Zimbabwe, headed by Prime Minister Robert Mugabe.

ZAPU – Zimbabwe African People's Union, party headed by Joshua Nkomo.

I have learnt
from books dear friend
of men dreaming and living
and hungering in a room without a light
who could not die since death was far too poor
who did not sleep to dream, but dreamed to change the world.

from *Poems of Succession* by Martin Carter
(New Beacon Books)

Chapter 1

An enemy bent on utter destruction

Black Africa has been deformed by apartheid – its vitality weakened and wasted. Its connection to the rest of the world has dwindled as its shadow grows smaller and takes up less space in international concern. The white regime in South Africa in its struggle to survive has, over the last decade and more, spread death, economic destruction, starvation and division across the African continent, brazenly piling horror and illegality so high upon each other that the rest of the world has lacked an adequate vocabulary of outrage. The reality has been, as contemporaries found Hitler's Germany, too profoundly disturbing for the normal mind to comprehend. Only Mozambique's great artist Malangatana, the Gabriel García Márquez of painting, has expressed on his huge brilliant canvases the grotesquely disfigured and distorted faces of what has become everyday life in Africa.

Even Africa's leaders have chosen to hide their people's agony behind the stony clichés of diplomacy and the dress uniforms and three-piece suits that adorn the state houses of the former colonialists.

But millions of individuals – whose haunting, accusing, tortured eyes Malangatana sears into the brain – are victims of the bombs, tanks, assassinations, arson, sabotage and insidious destabilization which the South African regime has employed to retain its power across the region.

This ruthless rearguard fight to hold back the continent's progression to black majority rule – and the transfer of economic power it implies – has produced more than a decade of open and covert war in all the countries of Southern Africa. It is a largely invisible war, enacted in remote underpopulated bush, forest or farmland where 90 per cent of Africans live, barely touched by the outside world until South Africa brought it to them, devastating past harmonies and future hopes.

In the former Portuguese colonies of Angola and Mozambique, and to a lesser extent in Zimbabwe, Zambia, Lesotho, Botswana and Tanzania, the hopes of independence twenty years ago have been shattered. South Africa has spread war and destruction where peace and stability would have provided an opportunity to build new nations; in these, health, education and economic development could have been the norm. If such nations had ever flowered, white South Africa would have adapted or died long ago. A very conservative estimate of the cost of South Africa's actions in eight years of the grim 1980s alone is $60 billion across the region – a crude cash calculation which makes no allowance for human suffering, a consideration which any minor civil court would take into account as a matter of routine in Europe or the United States. Direct war damage to railways, roads and buildings bombed or mined in Angola alone was worth over $17 billion. Caring for refugees, the losses of production and exports from abandoned farms have cost another $1 billion plus. The total far exceeds all the foreign aid which went into the region in the same period. South Africa has thus forced its neighbours not just to stop developing but has actually unravelled the fabric of their societies.

South Africa could pay reparations many times over from the profits its backers take abroad every year, but black Africa has no muscle to force reparations – or even an end to the continuing violence – on to the world's agenda. Its former colonial masters, Britain, France, Belgium, West Germany and Portugal, do have the muscle, but have not wanted to use it. Although denouncing apartheid became fashionable in the mid-1980s, even in the ruling circles which are its main support, breaking the power of the white regime is strongly resisted. South Africa, like its ally Israel, is an important link in the web of Western domination of a region and of a continent.

The US, other Western countries, and South Africa itself have differing national interests and sometimes contradictory ones, but overall they share the same policy objectives. Their strategies and tactics have frequently merged across the gamut of open, covert and proxy wars, multiple economic pressures, and subtle forms of destabilization. Pretoria has not acted alone in its warping of a continent.

'This war is a cancer of imperialism,' said Lucio Lara, who was Angola's Chief of Party Organization for the first ten years of independence. He was one of Africa's inspirational leaders in the era of guerrilla wars of liberation against the armies of Portugal, the least sophisticated of the colonial powers. On this occasion he was talking to a congress of organized peasants about the war waged by South Africa's puppet movement, UNITA, and its leader, Jonas Savimbi in his own country in 1984.

It was a weekend in November 1984. For a whole day, in a small cinema in a poor provincial town, one of the country's powerful, Lara, was listening to the powerless. Peasants, chosen to speak by their own village organizations, described the harshness of their lives – no transport, no kerosene for lamps, no soap, no cloth, and worst of all no security. In the province of Malanje alone, 20,000 people were at that time displaced from their homes.

'We are facing an enemy bent on utter destruction,' said Lara.

This enemy wears the mask of UNITA; but it is none other than South Africa which destroys these bridges, these trains, these villages. Their objective is that tomorrow we will give up on this difficult situation and ask South Africa for peace. But we will never give in to Pretoria's demands. With our Cuban friends and other socialist friends we can resist – and we will. It is clear what our enemies want – they want to impose Savimbi on us. They want to force the MPLA to work with their yes-men. We never will, Savimbi is a traitor not just to Angola, but to all Africa.

Such straight-talking is deeply threatening to South Africa's attempt to break the will to resist, and to the West's call for conciliation in Southern Africa. Lucio Lara, no longer in the

Angolan MPLA's Political Bureau, though still in the Central Committee, has paid a high price for his clarity since the US openly marked him out as their worst enemy in Luanda and, indeed, the region. Like Fidel Castro, far away in Cuba, but an ever-present obsession for Washington in its policy towards Angola, Lucio Lara became for the Americans an individual target easier to focus on for an attack than the enormously popular ideology he represented.

Words, inspiring Africans to fight for their beliefs, have been the gift of men like Lucio Lara, Fidel Castro and a younger generation of African leaders such as Thomas Sankara of Burkina Faso and Yoweri Museveni of Uganda. The battles using tanks, aircraft, mines, mortars, grenades and guns are just part of the war against the forces of fatalism, racism and conservatism that seek to explain Africa's deepening misery as the inevitable product of its own errors, but subject to correction if only Africa would follow the prescriptions of Western institutions such as the World Bank and the IMF. The Western development industry, and the Live-Aid, Band-Aid phenomenon which grew out of its self-evident failure, would have it that the interests of the West and Africa can be reconciled. In fact, Africa's chaos, wars and economic failures are needed to underpin South Africa's justification for maintaining white minority rule and its attempt to dominate the continent from the south on behalf of its Western allies.

At Jonas Savimbi's UNITA headquarters in the south-east corner of Angola, under the protection of three South African air bases illegally installed in occupied Namibia, are banner slogans which encapsulate a decade or more of recent history: 'Russians, Czechs, Cubans, go home. UNITA, key to Angola. Angola, key to Africa. Africa, key to the West.' As Lucio Lara said, Savimbi is not just a traitor to Angola, but something much bigger, a traitor to Africa, a convenient Western-manipulated chink in the continent's armour of pride in independence and determination to choose the path of nationalism and socialism. Chou en Lai declared in a famous speech in 1964, after an extended tour of the continent, that Africa was ripe for revolution. He was right in his estimation of how many Africans feel, but wrong in his estimation of how ruthlessly the West would stave off such a threat.

The complicity of the United States, Britain and international agencies from the World Bank and IMF, through United Nations agencies like UNICEF to Christian missionary bodies, in the patterns of destruction which have crippled the continent's early years of independence is widely understood in Africa. Barely educated peasants, such as those in Malanje that weekend, who live with the harsh reality of the last decade's 25 per cent overall drop in income, used the conference breaks to discuss Savimbi, South Africa, and the role of the West, rather than their individual problems. This is due to the MPLA's effort in popular education, exemplified by men like Lucio Lara who never lose such opportunities to explain the roots of every day's hardship. Several hundred people had walked many hours to that congress – a testimony of faith in their own organization and in MPLA leaders like Lucio Lara, unbroken by the bitter disappointments of independence.

A little over a year later, as agricultural production continued to decline in Malanje, and the peasants witnessed more and more frequently their families or neighbours being mutilated by mines laid in their fields, the reality became clearer even to the rest of the world when the US openly gave more than $10 million worth of arms, including sophisticated Stinger missiles, to Jonas Savimbi's movement, UNITA. Like the 'contras' in Nicaragua, UNITA had become an open part of Washington's global scheme to re-establish Western, or US control where Third World nationalists with socialist ideals had won independence.

Meanwhile, thousands of miles away in Uganda, the same battle for control of the future was being fought with different arms. The Western aid agencies, led by UNICEF, and encouraged by a Western press campaign, sought control of the thousands of Ugandan children who had fought with Yoweri Museveni's National Resistance Army in Africa's first post-independence war of liberation. Schools and orphanages with traditional missionary-style education were proposed for these children, whose educational and political formation in the bush had produced a new social phenomenon in Uganda. The previous Ugandan elite, products of British civilian and military education, had crucified Uganda since independence. The West had backed them all, from the brutal Idi Amin, to the vicious and degraded neo-colonial regimes of Milton Obote after 1980, and then Tito Okello, as they fought a five-year civil war against Museveni. After Museveni's victory the West needed more subtle ways to re-establish influence in Kampala. Education, and aid to the vulnerable and dispossessed, were used here, as they have been consciously or unconsciously, in the Western battle for every part of Africa.

The United States, Britain, Israel, Portugal and West Germany have all supported South Africa in feeding the cancer of destruction. Africa's independence has been eroded by the buying and selling of arms, people and myths. All three have been crucial – the last, invisible, is perhaps the most deadly of destabilizers. Disinformation has been one of Pretoria's most successful weapons. Thanks to the Western media, uncritical consumers of disinformation and avid creators and sellers of myths, the rest of the world sees Africa as a continent of hopeless misery, famine, dictators and incompetence, to be patronized by armies of donors and experts. The picture is constantly pumped back into Africa, sapping self-confidence. But millions of Africans whose lives are shaped by the economic violence of the Western-based international financial system, as well as by emotional and physical violence, see more clearly than the Western media do a Western responsibility that has been callously ignored.

Colonialism left in Africa a bitter legacy of hatred against Europe. The first generation after independence was marked deeply with that hatred, however often it was disguised for reasons of prudence or courtesy. The second generation is less prudent, less courteous, and more desperate. In the struggle for physical survival in a world of empty shops, decaying hospitals, rising unemployment in towns, falling living standards in a countryside abandoned by its youth, communications and transport facilities dwindling, people feel their lives slipping away, their choices narrowing. There is a desperation that can only grow as material conditions worsen – as every reliable forecast says they will.

An increasing physical and intellectual effort has gone into the many-faceted struggle to subdue Southern Africa to white South Africa. The West – governments, international institutions, companies, media – has backed South Africa openly or covertly and thus added a new dimension to the old hatred of Europe.

Those long years when European missionaries, schoolmasters and colonial administrators successfully imposed their own attitudes on the African elite which stepped into their shoes at independence are over. The economic and social crisis of the continent in the last decade has squeezed most Europeans out of their key advisory positions in schools, ministries and presidencies. Many of the African generation which depended on these people and mimicked their attitudes and concerns have left the continent too. Some have taken refuge in the comforts of the international bureaucracy or Western business, dealing with Africa from a distance. Others are political or economic exiles struggling for personal or family survival. Others who understand the issue and still yearn for an independent Africa able to resist foreign domination are discouraged by the vastness of the task and go abroad.

The drain of the educated and talented out of Africa on a one-way ticket has ripped strength out of the continent. Powers of decision-making and analysis are reduced, and reduced further as communications worsen and the input of information becomes more random because of the foreign exchange shortages. These, in turn, produce shortages of books, papers and magazines. Even ministers often have no independent sources of information and must rely on the BBC World Service and the 'Voice of America' for news and analysis of their own region and its problems. Increasingly the field is left clear for Western explanations of the continent's crisis to become the accepted orthodoxy. Such explanations, usually written in the comfort of the International Monetary Fund or World Bank offices in Washington after a few hectic weeks in the ministerial suites and Hilton hotels of selected

African capitals, have a soothing blandness which masks the drama they forecast.

But, unseen, an intense fire of resistance burns in Africa today, well beyond what is visible in the civil war in the townships of South Africa. Copious reports by the aid donors and the World Bank highlight the alienation and despair to be found in the slums of Lagos and Accra, or the refugee camps of Sudan and Zambia. But they omit how clearly even the uneducated and dispossessed of Africa increasingly focus on Western governments' and institutions' policies as the source of their deepening crisis. The Westerner, whose impatient habits of mind leave him handicapped, semi-deaf or wrapped in a comforting ignorance, does not often take in this resistance to him and all he represents.

But a continental grapevine is in place. Deep in the Ugandan bush, for instance, in the early 1980s, the young guerrillas fighting the British-led and trained government army of President Milton Obote were inspired to achieve the impossible by the example of anti-colonial wars and leaders like Lucio Lara. And they knew, too, about an idealistic young francophone army captain called Thomas Sankara whose group had, against all predictions, brought a different kind of revolution to a more backward, obscure and remote neo-colonial country than their own.

On the first anniversary of his seizure of power in Upper Volta, a tiny land-locked country in West Africa, Sankara renamed the country Burkina Faso, a name which used two local languages and which meant 'country of upright citizens'. Much of the outside world, if they even knew, laughed, if a little uneasily, at the naïve young army captains with their symbols.

No one in Africa had trouble remembering the name.

Two months later Captain Sankara spoke at the United Nations and, quoting Fidel Castro's speech to the Non-Aligned Summit at New Delhi in 1983, made a powerful case for a 'right to development' for countries like Burkina, and linked it to a need for cuts in superpower arms spending. The link he made, between development and disarmament, so clear to most Third World leaders, is always rejected by US and many Western officials as threatening to their interests. That speech of Sankara's, his political début on a wider platform than a West African regional one, also marked the beginning of more serious attempts, generated externally, to destabilize the new politics of Burkina by coup attempts and a near-miss assassination attempt on the President during a visit to Ivory Coast in 1985.

In October 1987 they succeeded. A bloody coup staged by his own closest associates killed Sankara and set in motion the retreat of his challenge to the old elite in his country and their patrons in Ivory Coast and France. There were many in Africa who saw that death as of far wider significance than for Burkina itself. In Ghana there were seven days of official mourning with all flags at halfmast. In Brazzaville crowds demonstrated in the streets. In South Africa young people remembered Sankara's symbolic gift of ten rifles made the previous year as civil war gripped the black townships and the youth were clamouring for guns.

Behind the current struggle for power in South Africa, and for the soul of Southern Africa, much more is at stake than the fate of a white ruling class. It is a confrontation not between East and West, as the makers of US foreign policy would have it, but between the irreconcilable interests of the Western powers in maintaining their economic and ideological domination of the continent, and African demands for the basic human rights of food, health, education, housing, security and choices in life. At its roots is a battle of ideas about the shape of people's futures. As the brilliant Colombian novelist Gabriel García Márquez wrote of Latin America, but it could just as well have been of Africa, 'The continent neither wants nor has any reason to be just a pawn without a will of its own; there's no reason why its plans for independence and orginality could not become part of the aspirations of the West.'

Women, children and armies of Cunene

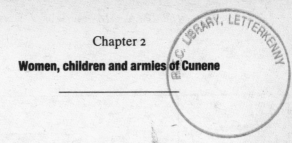

Ngiva in southern Angola was once a pretty little African town. Great herds of cattle grazed by the roadside under thorn trees during the day and in the evening wandered slowly home to compounds made of interlaced twigs and branches encircling small round earth-walled huts. In the centre of town bougainvillaea flowers sprouted scarlet, orange and pink from rich red earth and climbed in brilliant drifts over a courtyard. In its dappled shade children sat in disciplined rings singing, clapping and learning to count – education was the pride of Angola's early days of independence under Agostinho Neto's MPLA. Education was to be the new government's key to rapid transformation of an isolated and exploited medieval population. In rural areas like Ngiva and the surrounding province of Cunene peasants lived completely circumscribed by their own villages. An occasional violent eruption among them of Portuguese soldiers had for many people been the only contact with the colonial power. Through the 1960s, during the long war for independence, MPLA guerrillas in the remote villages of eastern Angola and the great dense forests of Cabinda painstakingly spread basic teaching of reading and writing even before they had military supplies physically to arm their supporters against the Portuguese colonial administration. The MPLA started education on a blank page. Portugal, of all the European colonial powers in Africa, did least to educate the black populations it ruled, in Angola, Mozambique, Guinea-Bissau, Cape Verde and São Tomé. The passivity and fatalism of the peasants were deliberately reinforced with a level of institutionalized brutality by the Portuguese military. Eventually the colonial power rotted from within and Portuguese fascism collapsed in Lisbon. Like the American soldiers

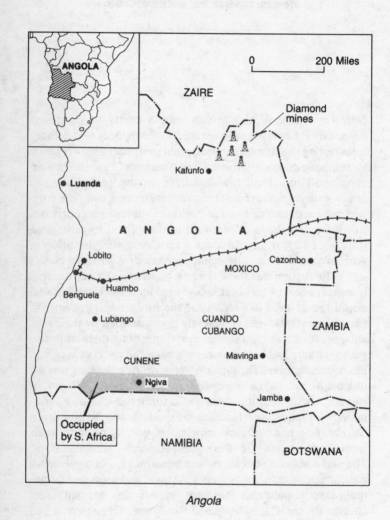

Angola

in Vietnam, the individual Portuguese soldiers had lost faith in their own myths of why they were in Africa. They simply gave up.

At independence Ngiva's style was that of a Portuguese provincial town. The slow-moving main street had a cinema, a bank, whitewashed one-storey government buildings with tin roofs, and a modest hospital. This peaceful normality of the late 1970s was a brief moment of harmony, a moment snatched between the violent slave labour of Portuguese colonialism and ruthless white South African violence. Independent Angola was to be held in thrall by South Africa for its wealth of oil and diamonds, and in order to humble the MPLA for daring to offer Africa the example of a successful non-racial, non-aligned state based on socialist principles. As the first echoes of the idea of Angolan independence began to reach the Portuguese powers in 1961, the colonialists, trying to stave off change, made educated and even semi-educated Africans a special target of repression. They had Angolan collaborators in this policy and an estimated 20,000 or more were murdered by the confused and transitory movement – the People's Union of Angola. So began a continuing brutality which raised barely a ripple in the outside world. Bertold Brecht's words could have been written for Angola then, and they still apply today: 'The first time it was reported that our friends were being butchered there was a cry of horror. Then a hundred were butchered. But when a thousand were butchered and there was no end to the butchery a blanket of silence spread. When evil-doing comes like falling rain, nobody calls out stop. When crimes begin to pile up they become invisible.'

Ngiva, deep in the Angolan bush, in the province of Cunene, which with neighbouring Kuando Kubango the Portuguese soldiers called the lands at the end of the earth, has been easy to cover with Brecht's blanket of silence.

In 1975 the kindergarten, the hospital and the fledgling administration thirty miles north of Namibia's border with southern Angola were overrun by South African tanks, trucks and artillery as Pretoria invaded the country in a bid to reach Luanda and prevent the MPLA taking power from Portugal on the planned independence day of 11 November. The majority of black Africa already recognized the MPLA, and the Cuban government made its historic decision to bring its own troops thousands of miles across the sea to hold back South Africa's military advance on Luanda. The history of today's destruction began then, as South Africa fought from the south, together with units of the Zaïrean army, to install in the place of the MPLA the CIA-funded UNITA and FNLA groups under Jonas Savimbi and Holden Roberto, who was related by marriage to Zaïre's President Mobuto Sese Seko. Mobuto himself had been installed by force in the 1960s, and maintained in power by the United States. Patrice Lumumba, the first elected nationalist leader to emerge in the Belgian Congo, now Zaïre, had been murdered five years earlier, to the undisguised relief of Washington. The series of CIA plans to murder him came out only later in Congress. Ngiva was occupied for the second time in 1981 by the South African military who set up camp there during the invasion known as Operation Protea. In the aftermath of the third invasion – Operation Askari starting in late 1983 and continuing in 1984 – it was razed to the ground with air-strikes and explosives placed in key targets, such as the bank and electricity generators. Then the South African tanks and huge armoured cars full of soldiers, black and white, rolled slowly southward towards the border, ending their occupation with an orgy of vengeful destruction, identical – but this time not filmed for Western television audiences – to Uganda's torment at the hands of the fleeing soldiers of Idi Amin in 1979 or the remnants of Milton Obote's and the short-lived venal Okello regime's armies in 1986. In the lands at the end of the earth the South Africans did not see the people as history's witnesses against them; they were black peasants with no leaders, invisible and voiceless to men who were themselves products of that mindless culture of control by violence – apartheid.

Just a few weeks after the bombing and burning of Ngiva, in October 1984, an Angolan military plane touched down at Ngiva's airport, a tarmac strip with one pock-marked crumbling building in a sea of tall pale grass and prickly scrub. Ngiva then was at the temporary truce line where the retreating South African army had halted on its way back to another war and another illegal occupation (of Namibia, the former German colony of South West Africa). Up the potholed track to the airstrip lumbered two South African armoured personnel carriers, the 'hippos' familiar to every viewer of television news film of police action in the South African townships. Sweating black soldiers peered out from inside. On top were two young white officers. With the defensive arrogance of every uneasy occupying army they stared in silence at the plane. No doubt their fantasies were of Soviet generals and Cuban advisers on board. Instead five women and an Angolan Air Force officer got out of the big jet, climbed into two waiting Angolan military jeeps and drove off into the shattered town.

Three of the women had been among the hundreds who had fled from Ngiva three years before when the South African military poured over the border in convoys and occupied Angola's Cunene province. In the silence of a baking afternoon these women looked without speaking at the ruins of their former lives. The courtyard where their Women's Organization had had its pre-school crèche was a heap of rubble. The hospital where some had had their babies had one wing left standing. Through the gaping hole in the wall of one ward the roof could be seen propped against the other wall. The town power-supply was a tangle of wires and cables. All that was left of a water-supply was a muddy pool on the outskirts of the town. The place had been devastated – Dresden on a small scale, it was a ghost town.

It was impossible to imagine normal life could start again in such a place. But a T-shirt drying on an overgrown rose bush, and a goat munching scarlet hibiscus flowers, showed that someone was living in one of the battered houses. Throughout the South African occupation some people had simply stayed on, scratching a subsistence living with a few cows or goats, sunk back to pre-colonial patterns – small lives of deep silence cut off from authorities or connections in the wider world.

Huge herds of cattle, the wealth of Cunene, were driven across the border into Namibia by the South Africans. For weeks the South African military camps in the Caprivi Strip and northern Namibia must have barbecued steaks around their swimming pools.

Overnight, for those Angolans who stayed, markets and veterinary services vanished along with the MPLA's infrastructure, which had organized education and health care and had promised Ngiva's people an identity as part of a nation. Instead Ngiva became a headquarters for the South African troops' probing attacks deep into Angola's villages on the pretext of searching for Namibia's black nationalists, SWAPO – those who were fighting for independence in Africa's last colony. Gradually southern Angola, like northern Namibia, became a huge no-go area in which those civilians who stayed risked house searches, house burnings, rapes, kidnappings and mysterious disappearances whenever a South African patrol happened on an isolated cluster of huts.

Among those South African troops, forever proving their virility by outdoing each other in brutality, were Portuguese soldiers, former Rhodesians, US and European mercenaries and Angolans. Some had been members of UNITA or FNLA or deserters from the MPLA who had fled south ten years before and then joined the South African army. By 1984 UNITA, led by Jonas Savimbi, was so closely linked into the South African regular army (SADF) that only the South African military command knew where one ended and the other began. The Angolans among the South African soldiers certainly did not know; they had been taught only to believe they were fighting Russians and Cubans for the future of Angola.

The first contact between Angolan government troops (FAPLA) and South African/Angolan troops during the truce of 1984 was so bizarre that it would have been funny if it had not spelt death so many times. Many Angolan soldiers from the South African side found relatives, friends or neighbours among the FAPLA soldiers who welcomed them with open arms. The first question from the Angolans on the South African side was always the same: 'Where are the Russian generals in command?' On that assumption these men had spent a decade killing their own people. The South African commanders, quick to scent a collapse of morale, exchanged the unit, within days, for one made up of Namibian bushmen.

Angola, by the mid-1980s, ten years after independence, often seemed to be a land of women. Deep in the villages and towns of rural areas like Cunene the mainspring of authority and continuity was the women, like the ones on the grim visit to Ngiva, deeply marked by so much experience of death and destruction and with such heavy responsibilities. Every war turns out women like this, but in Angola the extraordinary demands on women have been not temporary but the stuff of normal life for two decades.

The three women community leaders, who had seized that first opportunity to return to Ngiva, although the South African military were still on the edge of town, surveyed the desolation without a trace of self-pity. Before the afternoon was over they had begun to plan how to rebuild and bring back the women and children so hurriedly evacuated to government-controlled areas three years before.

In 1981 Angelina Carina was living in Ngiva where she worked as the co-ordinator of the government's Women's Organization in Cunene. In one day her work of organizing peaceful crèches, sewing groups and literacy classes, was transformed into an emergency war effort. Suddenly Angelina was having to cope with women and children traumatized by a night of South African bombing, followed by an early morning invasion of troops in armoured personnel carriers and jeeps. The South Africans began house-to-house searches for community leaders at once. Some of them had photographs of the people they were looking for, others were accompanied by collaborators, linked to UNITA, who identified people for them. Angelina organized a large group of women and children to dress as poor peasants and pose as looters rifling through abandoned homes. Her own strong intelligent face could easily have given them all away, but the disguises fooled the South African military and the group escaped northwards through South African lines in the course of the next few days.

As MPLA cadres like Angelina regrouped women and children, they had to deal with case after case of shock and trauma. So many women had been repeatedly raped and sexually tortured that they had appalling internal injuries. One small group of foreign nuns provided the only outside resource of emotional strength and modest medical facilities. They saw clearly and will never forget the hallmarks of South African and UNITA brutality on horribly mutilated children or pregnant women with their stomachs split open. There are mental scars and ineradicable hatreds across Cunene. The men did not much want to hear about these things then or now, but the women have never stopped talking among themselves of the nightmares which were only too real then and today are still not far from their thoughts.

The modest leaders of the MPLA Women's Organization (OMA), like the three in Ngiva that day, nursed and supported the traumatized women. They reorganized pathetic bands of tattered refugees and taught them again, as they had in the guerrilla war, to live with a long view of history. From nothing, and with sparse outside help, modest programmes of education and production of a few things like candles, pots and vegetables started up again in the camps where tens of thousands of displaced people were installed. The women used to make a particular kind of candle – golden and with an intricate lattice design of many layers built out from the core. It took infinite patience to get the thin wax strips to support the edifice, but then it burned for many weeks and months, like a symbol of their rebuilt organization.

By mid-1985 the South African army had withdrawn over the Namibian border – though it had taken them fifteen months to do so instead of the one month promised. But it was to be a brief respite. A force of 10,000 troops remained menacingly on the frontier, threatening Cunene. The SADF reinvaded with great waves of further destruction over three days in July and a week in October. By December their presence was semi-permanent again. Late in the year the MPLA Commander of the Fifth Military Region, Major Luis Faceira, gave an inventory of the South African forces in the area: 3 brigades, 18 infantry battalions and 2 assault battalions – about 20,000 men in all – 150 tanks, 400 artillery pieces, 300 mortars, several hundred armoured personnel carriers, 80 planes and helicopters. Throughout 1986 and 1987 the South Africans drove in and out across Cunene as they pleased, often killing or abducting the civilians or small FAPLA units that they came across.

Despite all this, Cunene's civilian population, homesick and lacking information about what might await them, or official encouragement, began, by about September 1985, to drift back into the province.

Everyone was used to such voids. Twelve months later Cunene was, from the air, no longer an empty landscape. A brown and greyish patchwork showed maize fields already harvested and the ground tilled for cassava and millet planting. Angelina Carina was back in the province and the first OMA meeting brought together 600 women determined to rebuild their family lives in the rubble of Ngiva and other similarly devastated towns. In the centre of Ngiva returned refugees had quietly moved into some of the least battered buildings. They were feeding themselves as best they could and performing miracles of self-sufficiency and co-operation as they worked on land which had returned to scruffy bush in their absence The South African occupiers had lived with supplies in plenty trucked in or dropped in by air. A skeleton MPLA administration was slowly put in place. Some authority filled the vacuum, but resources were non-existent.

Hundred of miles to the north, in Luanda, a commission for the rehabilitation of ravaged Cunene was proposed by President Eduardo Dos Santos. It was to be headed by Rui de Sa, known as 'Dibala', a guerrilla veteran of the equally difficult days of the liberation war period in the deep Cabinda forest, and in Lunda in the east where he was political commissar from 1970–4. Aid donors wrote project reports, consultants were paid for them. But it was all theoretical. The collapse of the oil price in early 1986 killed even the theory of rehabilitation. And the increased aggression by South Africa in and from Namibia throughout 1987 deferred reconstruction further – until after the fall of the white regime in Pretoria, many Angolans believed.

But, far away across the world another generation of Angolans and Namibians were being educated for Cunene's future. Hundreds of the children who lost everything except their own lives in the devastation were taken to Cuba and given experiences and ideals as diametrically opposed as it is possible to imagine from those white South Africa and its allies live by

The Portuguese colonialists deliberately deprived Angolans of education. Just as deliberately the MPLA put its own and its allies' resources into education which would transmit the values and ideology behind the war of independence.

The Island of Youth, a short flight off the mainland of Cuba, is extravagantly lush. A wide, well-maintained tarmac road winds between orange groves, high grass and dairy cattle grazing in neatly fenced pastures. Across a bridge, a bend in the river gives a glimpse of a group of children swimming and canoeing with shrieks of laughter. Beside the road a row of huge portraits looms up on billboards – Fidel Castro, Agostinho Neto and Eduardo Dos Santos of Angola, Joachim Chissano of Mozambique, Sam Nujoma of Namibia, Oliver Tambo and Nelson Mandela of South Africa. The road approaches the extraordinary schools where Southern Africa's children, so deeply wounded in spirit and so deeply deprived in body, are being given an education equal to the best they could receive in any other continent. They will be their countries' leaders who shape the continent for a future very different from the downward spiral of famine, debt, decapitalization, educational deprivation, and degradation from which the post-independence African leaders have been unable to escape.

Many of the children from Cunene are in the school run for the Namibian independence movement, SWAPO. The school is a three-storey whitewashed building with wide steps leading to a front hall decorated with bright pots of flowering plants. At the top of the steps a group of large teenagers waited to greet the visitors. The first stunning impression for anyone coming from the devastated wastelands of Southern Angola is of the exuberant confidence, health and spirits of these children, singing a welcome, shaking hands, leading the visitors to find a SWAPO teacher.

One of the Cuban teachers, looking at the articulate six-foot boy leading the way to a permanent exhibition of historical drawings, paintings and home-made artefacts of Namibia, remembered the skinny, scarred eleven-year-old who arrived at the school in rags in 1978. That child was one of the survivors of South Africa's invasion and massacre of Namibian refugees in Southern Angola at Kassinga. 'They were all so small, so terrorized, so silent, you would have imagined they would be permanent emotional cripples.'

The central force of every child's life in this school is their response to what happened to them on 4 May 1978. A large handsome boy at a desk at the back of the classroom volunteered to tell the story. 'It was early, about 7, and we were at the camp morning meeting before school when planes suddenly appeared and I saw bombs fall out of them. People began screaming and running but some bits of people were all around us on the ground. Then white soldiers, some shouting in Portuguese, seemed to come from everywhere out of the bush.' Other children went on with the story calmly. It has been told so many times that the traumatic wounds seemed to have healed miraculously in their minds. 'Some people climbed into trucks, but they blew up as they tried to drive out of the camp. Some soldiers shot people in the face looking at them. Or they kicked them over and stuck bayonets in them.' Listening to these children carefully explaining the inexplicable the mind slides away from understanding what is meant.

A journalist who arrived in Kassinga the day after the massacre wrote of the 'brightly coloured cotton frocks of the young girls, jeans, checked shirts of the boys, a few khaki uniforms and swollen bodies of the dead. The victims were mostly very young and had no defence.'

At that time Kassinga was SWAPO's main transit centre and settlement. It lies north of Ngiva, 250 kilometres inside Angola in deserted bush country. There were 4,098 refugees from Namibia living in iron mine buildings, and tents. The refugees were men, women and children who had walked hundreds of kilometres through the bush in terror to escape the South Africans' violence, both physical and psychological. Some had been arrested, imprisoned, tortured, released; others had seen family members taken from their homes never to return; still others had been paid, flattered or bullied into promising to work for the South Africans. Kassinga's modest facilities, provided by the UN refugee agency UNHCR and Angola, included a school, a sewing factory and truck repair works. There was no military camp. The refugees had built on this fragile normality ordinary small dignified lives and a thriving sense of community. As one of them said later, 'We felt free, safe, happy – it was a kind of introduction to our own independence which we thought was rather near.'

That day, in an attempt to incite SWAPO into breaking off UN-sponsored independence negotiations (see Chapter 5), the South Africans invaded Angola from their illegal bases in occupied Namibia using twelve Mirage jets, four Hercules troop carriers, five helicopters and sixty armoured cars. It was the same kind of wholly disproportionate force which the US used in the 1986 bombing attack on the Libyan capital, Tripoli. But, being far from the world's attention, the civilian casualties raised barely a murmur of indignation. Truly, in the lands at the end of the earth, as the Portuguese found, guns could make any shape of history they liked and no one would know.

More than 600 Namibians were killed and later buried by the Angolans in great mass graves soon covered by long pale grass. The South African commanders, safe inside their jets and armoured cars, ordered wholesale arrests of survivors 'for interrogation'. Soldiers bundled 118 people, including 40 women, into planes and took them back to prison and torture in Namibia. Refugees numbering 1,500 were left behind wounded. They stayed among the dead all day until they could be evacuated to hospital in Luanda. Long after the camp's buildings and tents lay flat amid the dead or dying, South African planes continued bombing in waves. All day the Angolan army (FAPLA) attempted to reach Kassinga's survivors. Air strikes against the FAPLA column trying to advance killed 16 soldiers and wounded 74.

Within weeks 600 children, mostly traumatized orphans, were flown away from the nightmare memories of Kassinga to Cuba's Island of Youth. These survivors are a moving testimony to the resilience of the human spirit. In five years the school had miraculously produced people who saw themselves as future pilots, doctors, teachers and engineers. Their educational grounding from Namibia was virtually nil. Infant mortality among black children in that potentially rich country is eight times that of white. Child malnutrition is as severe as in

Ethiopia and Sudan, bad enough to threaten lifelong brain damage and, certainly, physical stunting. Even basic primary education is a privilege of only 10 per cent of black children. In SWAPO's Kassinga camp there was rudimentary schooling for all, financed from the slender resources the international community offers to a liberation movement fighting for its life.

In the Cuban school on the Island of Youth the children exude a rare sense of self-discipline and pride. Every child has been imbued with an unyielding sense of common purpose and responsibility: to work for the Namibian liberation struggle and then to build a nation from scratch. Like the awesome women in the SWAPO leadership who long ago learned to live with the ache of missing children away at boarding schools all year round and husbands distant in the war front, these children possess an astonishing strength and selflessness. Their experiences have taught them to believe in vengeance, not for their own trauma of Kassinga and all that preceded it in South African-occupied Namibia, but for their whole country enslaved and cowed by Pretoria, milked of its uranium and diamond riches by Western countries, its injustices largely forgotten by the rest of the world – apart from a ritualized annual expression of dismay at the United Nations General Assembly every autumn. Their education has taught them not the resignation and individualism Western mission schools offered Africans, but a tough pride and high aspirations for the collective advance of their communities and countries.

One boy says quietly that he will train as a pilot so that he can kill South Africans. Several girls say they will be teachers so that the next generation will better understand world economics and history, and will know why the West put its weight behind Pretoria, rather than Namibia and justice.

These children so far away from the African mainstream were symbols of the depth of impending change in Southern Africa. With every escalation of resistance to the white regime in the townships of South Africa itself during 1985 and 1986 the echoes in Europe were heard more clearly. Elder statesmen from the Commonwealth visited Nelson Mandela in prison and President Botha in Pretoria, seeking dialogue and compromise. American businesses began to pull out of South

Africa; all over the world popular imagination ran far ahead of political developments to make Nelson Mandela a familiar father-figure and popular hero. South African exiles formed a strong sub-culture in London's music world and infused liberation politics into it with a very successful song of homage to Mandela. In the summer of 1984 an open-air concert in London for the South African hero's sixty-fifth birthday packed the vast grounds of the Alexandra Palace and para-lysed the traffic in the area throughout the day. The South African trumpeter Hugh Masekela became a cult figure whose concerts sold out all over Europe. In the wake of the police killings at Uitenhage in 1985 on the anniversary of the Sharpeville massacre, Masekela played in a big London hall, his white shirt soaked through with sweat, face glistening with exhaustion as the audience roared for encore after encore in a great outpouring of emotion. A year later, in the summer of 1986, Masekela's trumpet notes wafted right across Clapham Common to a crowd far outnumbering any political gathering on issues closer to home. It was a different audience and a different emotion from Geldof's politics of pity for poor Africans endorsed by Buckingham Palace.

Over the years of his imprisonment on Robben Island Mandela had become an indissoluble part of every black political experience – for those who had never been to Africa as well as for Africa's own intellectual leaders. He was the unifying figure who bestraddled the sectarian splits that para-lysed so many of Africa's intellectuals and their various movements of resistance to the status quo on their continent. Mandela's refusal of the conditional offers of freedom made by the white regime increased his stature even further. At London's Black Book Fair in 1985 the Nigerian writer Wole Soyinka paid a moving tribute to Mandela's leadership from behind bars, contrasting it with the policies of some of the continent's prominent leaders. During that same Book Fair, across the city in Brixton, the young Caribbean poet Lorna Goodison read her poem on the South African police arresting Winnie Mandela's bedspread to cheers, applause and laughter from an audience who had mostly experienced Africa, like her, only in the imagination:

They arrested the bedspread.
They and their friends are working
to arrest the dreams in our heads
and the women, accustomed to closing
the eyes of the dead
are weaving cloths still brighter.

Chapter 3

Dividing the continent

Divide and rule is the oldest and most successful formula for all imperial, colonial and neo-colonial powers. Division has been the great weakener of post-colonial Africa, killing the dreams of regional industrialization and of a unified anti-imperialist basis for external policy that Kwame Nkrumah formulated in Ghana from the moment he led the country to independence from Britain in 1956. As the colonial powers granted independence to one African country after another they tried to ensure that power went to an elite who would reject socialism, and even nationalism, and who would maintain Western influence in all domains. But Nkrumah would be the first of many to set a different tone – one of vibrant nationalism for the whole continent. In 1958 he hosted the first Conference of Independent African States in Accra. There were then only eight members – Morocco, Tunisia, Libya, Egypt, Sudan, Ethiopia, Liberia and Ghana. For the first time these African states declared themselves a unified group, 'the vanguard for the complete emancipation of Africa', Nkrumah wrote; 'the continental struggle for Africa's total liberation from imperialism and neo-colonialism has begun.'

Before the end of that year Nkrumah had hosted another conference, that of all freedom movements and political parties on the continent. That All-African People's Conference in December 1958 brought together unknown men from British, Portuguese and French colonies who, within a decade of the feverish power struggles associated with independence, would be presidents, prime ministers, and party leaders – men like Julius Nyerere, Kenneth Kaunda or Rashid Karume, and some of the continent's losers like Patrice Lumumba, Jaramogi Oginga Odinga, and Joshua Nkomo. South Africans

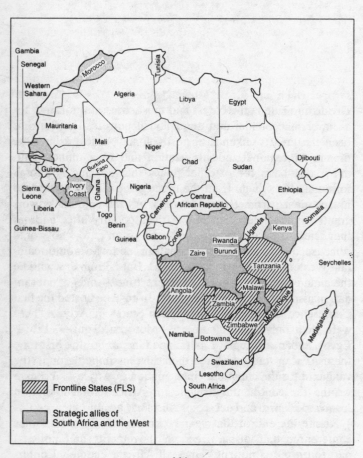

Africa

were then one group among many seeking liberation. 'My object', said Nkrumah, 'was to infuse into the African Revolution new spirit and a new dynamism; and to create these where they were lacking. The Conference was to sound the clarion call for the advance and final assault on imperialism and the complete eradication of colonial oppression in Africa.'

Nkrumah meanwhile was searching for new economic patterns for his country, and specifically connections in Eastern Europe which could free Ghana from the West's power of price-fixing in the all-important cocoa trade. Years later the man who had been responsible for the mission to Eastern Europe to try to set up a barter deal for part of the cocoa harvest, Amoako-Attah, still believed that an economic deal with Eastern Europe, and the new relationships it would mean, could have worked. In his last year, in spite of illness, Amoako Attah advised the new Ghanaian regime of Flight Lieutenant Rawlings not to enter the IMF and World Bank's 'clinging web of unseen constraints'.

Immediately after launching the economic opening to the socialist bloc Nkrumah was overthrown. It had been a widely anticipated coup. Members of the army and police struck on 24 February 1966 while he was on the way to Hanoi, carrying proposals which he hoped could end the Vietnam war. The conspiracy against him by members of the armed forces and police had begun the previous summer and the CIA was closely informed of its progress by Police Commissioner John Harley, the key member of the coup group. It was a classic case, like the even more tragic one of Lumumba's death in the Congo, of internal forces being sufficiently assured they would obtain moral and material support from imperialism after the event, to move against a nationalist leader with a continent-wide following. Rewards, especially in the economic field, were immediate.

The Western powers greeted the replacement of Nkrumah by a pro-Western military junta with an immediate granting of £20 million in standby facilities from the IMF. Britain in particular warmly embraced the new Ghanaian government that so neatly reversed Nkrumah's foreign and economic policy directions, starting with restoring diplomatic relations with Britain, which Nkrumah had cut in protest over Rhodesia. The US immediately sent food aid, which had been refused to Nkrumah. West Germany negotiated a twenty-year loan. The International Confederation of Free Trade Unions brought advisers into the trade union movement.

The wider issue of the threat Nkrumah's ideas had posed to the West was masked by the history of the period, rapidly being rewritten by journalists, both inside the country and abroad. The visionary who had inspired a generation to fight for the freedom and unity of the continent was reviled and redrawn to resemble US Ambassador William Mahoney's picture of a leader who was no more than 'a mixed up kid . . . insecure . . . plagued with inward uncertainty and forever searching for simple answers to problems he poorly understands'. (This is from Ambassador Mahoney's Year-End Assessment for Department of State, 10 January 1964, Secret Ref, CERP C-1, CA-5084, CA-6355.)

The United States, Israel and the former colonial powers Britain, France, Portugal and West Germany have, in pursuit of their own goals, particularly in South Africa, been the source of most of Africa's internal violence and the continent's divisions in the post-independence decades, although these divisions are generally presented in the West as natural phenomena. The conventional wisdom of the West divides Africa by tribe, religion, and on the basis of the colonizing powers' languages, into francophone, anglophone and Portuguese-speaking.

But the real divisions are other; Africa's leaders can broadly be classified by the economic and political dependence or independence they have sought. In the economic sphere the motors of dependence are the World Bank and the International Monetary Fund whose patterns of economic development have defined so much of the continent. Countries which accepted the Bank and Fund prescriptions for development early on, and which therefore found Western capital forthcoming form one distinct group. They include Ivory Coast, Morocco, Kenya, Sudan (under Nimeiri), Egypt, Senegal, Malawi and Zaïre. Without exception the ruling elites of this group have personal fortunes in property and foreign bank accounts, which are so immense they may, as in the case of Zaïre, equal the entire national debt. For instance, President Mobutu in 1982 spent $2 million on taking an entourage of ninety-three people to Disney World in Florida by chartered plane – an incident which aptly demonstrated this Head of State's style of spending and tastes.

Development capital from the West has not produced for these countries clean water, health care, primary schools and rural roads, but rather, biddable client leaders with business interests. These governments have been the West's proxies in blocking moves by more independently minded leaders for joint economic action – such as debt repudiation – which alone could force international action on Africa's dramatic economic weakness. Their own dependence has also made these Western-leaning states pliable partners with the West in its weakening of many currents of nationalist and socialist thinking in Africa, especially in Southern Africa. The key principle of supporting Africa's wars of independence, from Western Sahara to Namibia and South Africa, which was enshrined in the continent's historical self-definition by Nkrumah, has been under constant attack, usually veiled, by these allies of the West in Africa.

By early 1987, the continental economic crisis was threatening the meagre social gains made in every African country. Across the continent incomes had fallen by 15 per cent over five years. No fewer than twenty-five countries – almost half the continent – had begun to implement the Bank and Fund's drastic economic reform measures. These were intended to qualify them for World Bank finance under the Special Facility for Africa, which was set up in 1985 when the real depths of the coming impoverishment began to be seen. (At that time only ten countries were expected to apply for it.)

Among the twenty-five were several candidates unlikely to become World Bank models. Informally grouped, they are among those which had tried for a decade or so to define their own economic agenda, usually based precisely upon agricultural self-sufficiency and community-organized initiatives. Invariably they found that their resistance to Bank and Fund prescriptions that they should increase export crops, and cut urban purchasing power etc., put a brake on most other bilateral and multilateral capital inflows. Scandinavia, which for some years was prepared to follow its own social democratic instincts and provide aid to countries such as Tanzania and Ethiopia, changed tack around 1985 and in a mood of disillusion began to question its own criteria. Following a US trend, 'human rights' considerations became part of aid policy-making even in Scandinavia. The image of countries such as Tanzania which the West, for quite other, political, reasons had already begun to criticize, became suddenly tarnished by unchecked and frequently false allegations of human rights violations. Overnight 'human rights' had become another strand in the web of Western controls over Africa's access to resources.

The United States dominates decision-making in both the Bank and the Fund, just as the two organizations, which work increasingly as a double act with cross-conditions, dominate a wide range of donor attitudes. Western European aid officials' intermittent attempts at some independence from US positions are usually more cursory than they admit. And Washington's attitudes across the board, from the development agencies through the State Department to the White House, though not precisely monolithic, are rarely in flat contradiction and usually complement each other.

Such establishment attitudes meant that Ethiopia after Haile Selassie, Angola and Mozambique in the first decade after independence, Uganda since President Museveni came to power, and Burkina Faso, all suffered extreme difficulty in obtaining mainstream international funding for their own development priorities. In 1987 the decisions of Mozambique and Angola to join the IMF were a recognition that without the IMF's stamp of approval it was virtually impossible to play a real part in the world economy.

Access to the leadership within these countries became easier for Western government officials thanks to the Bank and Fund. They used it to press orthodox economic ideas, to widen differences, and to spread disinformation. Destabilization, which all suffered as a constant fact of life, had a new and more subtle introduction through the economy. In parallel, State Department officials were already involved in the co-opting of individuals or trying to buy into these various regimes in the hope of pushing for a change in character. The CIA and other Western intelligence services, were similarly active in encouraging a pro-Western line.

One of the particular targets for these manoeuvres was Ethiopia. The military regime known as the Derg which overthrew an important US African ally, the Emperor Haile Selassie, endured a mixture of economic and political pressures from the US in the early 1980s. Ethiopia's post-revolutionary leaders headed by Colonel Mengistu Haile Mariam had called on Cuban troops and Soviet military advisers to repel the Somali attempt to take over the Ogaden. Eritrean nationalists, once supported by the socialist bloc against Emperor Haile Selassie, and Tigrean dissidents, obtained US food aid and substantial secret Saudi support.

Other dissidents not strong enough to have a real chance of winning power, but an effective source of destabilization and disinformation about Ethiopia, were funded by the CIA. For instance the Ethiopian People's Democratic Alliance (EPDA), a London-based pliable conservative group, was opposed to the Derg, but had little following. From 1981 Reagan authorized a $500,000-a-year CIA programme of anti-Derg propaganda assistance to the EPDA through a network of cells in the Ethiopian capital. On 20 December 1983 the EPDA's CIA contact was arrested when caught red-handed with anti-Derg leaflets, hidden in a cupboard in an apartment in Addis Ababa. He was released the following February after a personal visit to the Ethiopian capital by General Vernon Walters, then the Reagan administration's roving envoy.

In this period US officials, from the President down, began to mention Ethiopia in the same breath as Angola, Afghanistan, Nicaragua and Kampuchea as countries where US military aid to 'freedom fighters' had a legitimate place. It was an ominous warning to the Derg of the possibility of a long stalemated war which could loom ahead.

Congressional hearings later indicated that in the same period the administration had taken advantage of Ethiopia's terrible famine to exacerbate destabilizing pressure on the Derg. Emergency food aid was sent to rebel-held areas in

Tigre by USAID in Sudan and was withheld from the Ethiopian government in Addis Ababa for more than a year after the full extent of the famine was well known to the international community there. American diplomats made no secret of their hope that the new famine would split the ruling military group along East/West ideological lines and so bring down the Derg, just as the previous one had hastened the end of the Emperor's regime. The delayed response was no accident. It not only killed untold numbers of Ethiopian peasants, but also, because of the magnitude of the disaster which the government was unable to cope with, weakened the Derg's political hold on the country. The regime's very survival was a surprise to many, and particularly to the US, which had groomed a government in waiting from the highly educated defectors to whom they had had access. It was US policy to cultivate officials inside the regime at the same time. The Americans hoped that the Derg's Marxism–Leninism was so shallowly rooted that a handful of men could engineer a rejection of the country's dependence on the Soviet Union's massive arms supplies and on the Cuban soldiers who guarded Addis Ababa's most important garrison. They sought a renewal of the strong ties which America had enjoyed with Emperor Haile Selassie's regime. Before the military took over Africa's last feudal system the US had an important communications base at Kagnew, which they could not have easily replaced in a neighbouring country.

But in the struggles for influence which still shook Addis Ababa periodically in the early 1980s, when the Derg had consolidated after earlier more bloody struggles, the pattern was invariably the reverse of the US plans. Doubting Ethiopian officials such as Major Dawit Wolde-Giorgis, Head of the Relief and Rehabilitation Commission, or Colonel Wolde Goshu, the Foreign Minister, always lost the battle for change and, amid much bitterness, left the country. In the process the Derg was weakened, some of its best minds lost, its base narrowed. Ethiopia's chance of transforming its impoverished feudal economy was deliberately withheld by lack of Western capital, when, ironically, its central economic development strategy was precisely the resettlement of thousands of peasants on more fertile land which the World Bank had earlier, under Haile Selassie, identified as the best plan for the country.

Although stopping short of causing the collapse of the Derg, US policies in Ethiopia had effectively postponed the emergence of a confident and successful radical African nationalist regime that could help the liberation movements further south on the continent, and serve as an encouraging model.

The pattern of interference, by economic coercion or even coup attempts, in any flowering of independent nationalism, has been repeated in numerous African countries. Even insignificant tiny countries have not been left alone in this post-independence period. One clear-cut case was the South African-financed attempted coup in November 1981 against President Albert René's far from radical regime in the Seychelles. It was led by the former Congo mercenary Mike Hoare, a resident of South Africa. Hoare himself published an account of South Africa's involvement in what he believed was an anti-communist enterprise with the political backing of the West. In the Comoro Islands and Mauritius too, radical regimes were overturned with guns, or money. Like the Seychelles, their nationalist governments backed the idea of the Indian Ocean as a zone of peace – a position the US strongly objected to.

Within the Washington establishment itself the Bank and the Fund have had some differences of opinion on the strength of their prescriptions, though not on the analysis of ailing African economies. Some Bank economists favoured softer conditions and were more afraid of the possible consequences of the urban unrest that often followed imposition of the classic IMF prescriptions: devaluation, cutting of subsidies on food and petrol, turning of state enterprises over to the private sector (usually multinational not indigenous capital) and pruning of jobs in the public sector. The drastic cutting of urban living standards which these measures involve can put a regime's survival in jeopardy, as riots after price rises showed in countries such as Egypt, Tunisia, Morocco, Sudan, Liberia and Zambia between 1975 and 1986.

By the mid-1980s the whole continent's economic crisis was

chronic, largely because of the drop in the world prices of commodities – a staggering $19 billion was lost in export earnings between 1985 and 1986 – which coincided with the rise in prices of oil and manufactured goods that Africa imported. Following heavy borrowing for development spending in the easier period before the oil price shock, debt servicing for many African countries was often consuming more than half their export earnings. From 1985 Africa made a net transfer of capital to the West of $2 billion a year. There was clearly no leeway for gradual measures to boost production, in the hope of reviving economies and paying off some debts, without a massive new injection of capital from Europe, the United States or Japan. No such capital was forthcoming and even bilateral loans became dependent on agreement with the IMF, as Tanzania discovered with the Scandinavians in 1986 and Mozambique and Zambia with Britain in 1987. The dream of a New International Economic Order launched in Algeria in the period of Boumedienne, and an inspiration to many poor nations in the mid-1970s, had died by the early 1980s.

Tanzania, home of the socialist Arusha Declaration of 1967, which fired a generation of nationalist economists across Africa, was, two decades later, the best-known example on the continent of an early Bank/Fund disagreement. Ghana in the mid-1980s was another. In both instances the Fund's drastic conditions for new loans prevailed in the end, with significant political consequences. Tanzania's capitulation to the Fund in 1986, after President Nyerere stepped down, showed that a six-year battle against Fund conditions had to be abandoned when the political space to fight it was no longer there. Ex-President Nyerere left the Indian Ocean capital to build the party organization at Dodoma in the great barren central plains of Tanzania. And as though to mock his twenty-year-old Arusha Declaration of Socialism, the Bank's trade liberalization rapidly changed the image of Dar Es Salaam's sparsely filled shops; videos and washing machines came in with the help of a small elite in the bureaucratic bourgeoisie allied to Zanzibari and Gulf-based trading families.

Fabian socialist and Christian leaders of Tanzania and Zambia were treated by the US as enemies because of their membership of the Front-line States and support for the African National Congress. Draconian economic austerity programmes imposed by the IMF jeopardized their popular urban support base.

Even a country well beyond the Front-line States with aspirations to radical nationalism at home and a policy of open support for the ANC's armed struggle, was subject to a merciless economic squeeze from Washington, which modified the regime's policies at home and abroad. The Ghanaian government of Flight Lieutenant Jerry Rawlings was too weak both politically and economically to withstand IMF prescriptions for more than a matter of months in 1982–3. The urban working class, particularly the fairly well-organized labour in the port of Tema, was then the critical support base for Rawlings' second military regime following a coup in December 1981. 'People's Power' was the slogan of posters and rallies every day. But the IMF/Bank programmes formulated from 1983 to 1985 specifically demanded that the ruling Provisional National Defence Council (PNDC) dismantle the local committees known as the Committees for the Defence of the Revolution at workplaces and community level. These fledgling democratic fora had provided political education and a fragile framework of organization from which People's Shops, primary health care and some self-management in industry were spontaneously growing. There were massive street demonstrations by workers in favour of the government, following a series of failed coups against Rawlings, and in favour of a harsh budget which they actually supported against middle-class and student attacks. Thus Ghana in 1982 and early 1983 presented a spectacle of working-class power (albeit more spontaneous than systematic) previously unseen in post-independence Africa. Only anti-colonial demonstrations of the Nkrumah era had had a similar mobilizing effect.

Rawlings, a populist, who initially had an enormous following among the impoverished and politically dispossessed urban working class, inherited, to the alarm of the West, Nkrumah's symbolic continental anti-imperialist leadership. Rawlings twice overthrew corrupt and incompetent governments in Ghana, in 1979 and 1981. The first was military, the second civilian. Both were neo-colonial regimes deeply dependent on the West economically and ideologically, and alienated from a population brutalized by plummeting living standards and the decay of health and educational institutions.

The US embassy in Accra was the centre for an elaborate network of CIA spies, exposed in 1983, 1984 and 1985 by the Ghanaian government and expelled from the country. The US was deeply involved in a long series of failed coups, plots, assassination attempts, and incursions from its regional allies such as Liberia, Nigeria, Togo and Ivory Coast, which kept Ghana in a state of destabilization. At the same time Washington and London together worked to force the regime into accepting the terms of the IMF and the World Bank whose loans were necessary to keep the country from bankruptcy. As the IMF imposed devaluation after devaluation on Ghana in 1984–6, in return for long-term and probably unrepayable loans, the cost of living rose so steeply in urban areas that the government was several times faced with near revolt by its own historic support base. The 1982 threat of the Rawlings government backing workers' takeovers of Western businesses, or a real revival of Nkrumah's plans for Pan-African economic programmes independent of Western control receded swiftly. By the end of 1986 Ghana was operating a model IMF economic austerity programme which involved the repression of popular democracy. As a symbol of African nationalism Rawlings' Ghana, like Tanzania under Julius Nyerere, as Ethiopia under Colonel Mengistu, had been rendered almost as impotent as Mozambique and Angola.

In both Tanzania and Ghana the political repercussions of accepting the IMF's terms were, for internal reasons, glossed over. President Nyerere of Tanzania was one of the few people who spelt out the implications of such IMF agreements. Firstly, the government was effectively ceding part of the country's sovereignty and political power to the Washington institutions; secondly, the government would, almost inevitably, be obliged to use force against its own citizens to maintain public order in the face of democratic protest against cuts in living standards.

Both Tanzania and Ghana witnessed examples of this unrest during 1986, though in both cases the incidents were largely hushed up. In Tanzania workers on a government sugar plantation at Kilombero were killed by security forces during a demonstration against the loss of allowances. In Ghana similar demonstrations were defused in early 1986 by a nervous government reversal of IMF-imposed cuts in civil service bonuses. Tanks, though, were brought out to surround the Trade Union Congress headquarters. It was a dramatic symbol of the change in the country's political atmosphere from late 1982 when, amid much greater worker turmoil, Rawlings drove up to the TUC building in an armoured personnel car, jumped out virtually alone, and for an hour or more talked intensely to a receptive crowd of extremely impoverished workers about the power of education and organization to change their lives. In just four years, as austerity bit deeper, Rawlings had lost his audience, and, it appeared, his confidence in his old-style popular debate.

Thus Western economic strategy towards regimes to which the West is hostile, fits neatly on to the political divisions and reinforces them. The same struggle for pre-eminence between Western-style and nationalist currents, as appears more starkly in the Southern African conflict, lay behind the widening of political and economic divisions throughout the continent. Allies of the West, like Zaïre or Nimeiri's Sudan, saw their debts rescheduled and credit lines extended indefinitely. To some extent at least their governments were cushioned from the political consequences of the ravages of needless deaths and progressive impoverishment which threatened to sweep others away.

In the early 1980s the continental grouping, the Organization of African Unity, heir of Nkrumah's initiatives, aptly illustrated the continent's searing political divisions when it nearly broke into two halves. Meetings at summit, ministerial and technical level were paralysed. The invisible US role in this damaging affair was crucial. A convenient simple focus of blame for long-standing and deep-rooted political division was found by the US and vigorously fostered by the Reagan administration – Colonel Gaddafy of Libya.

In fact Libya's importance in the near OAU split was wildly exaggerated by the US in their anxiety to try to prevent the diplomatic isolation of one of its most important African allies, Morocco. At issue in the OAU's acrimonious deliberations was the admittance into the organization of the Saharan Arab Democratic Republic (SADR), a tiny desert country on the west coast of Africa bordering Algeria, Morocco and Mauretania. The territory had fewer than a million inhabitants, its only resources were phosphate, of which there was a world glut, and fish. By its very nature it was hardly a likely candidate to become the focus of interest of the rest of Africa. It never would have become so without the deep US involvement with Morocco, lynchpin of the US axis in Africa, running through Egypt, Sudan, Zaïre, Kenya, Senegal, Liberia, Ivory Coast and Malawi.

The Western Sahara, formerly a Spanish colony, was ceded to Morocco and Mauretania in a secret deal (in which the inhabitants were not consulted) made while General Franco lay on his deathbed and Spanish politics were in disarray. In late 1975 King Hassan of Morocco had ordered a dramatic 'Green March' of hundreds of thousands of Moroccan citizens who set up their tents in the inhospitable sand wastelands of the Western Sahara. The civilian march camouflaged the massive deployment of the Moroccan army in the territory and effectively pre-empted a UN mission there which was about to declare in favour of independence for the Saharouis. The Moroccan move also ignored a ruling by the International Court of Justice in the Hague that the principle of self-determination must be applied, with the Saharouis themselves voting on the shape of their future. Such an exposed stance as Morocco's in international affairs could not have been taken with impunity by any Third World country without encouragement from Washington. In fact, General Vernon Walters, Deputy Director of the CIA, and Alfred Atherton, a senior official in Henry Kissinger's foreign policy entourage, went, respectively, to Spain and Morocco in this period of tension and disarray in Spanish/Moroccan relations. The last Spanish colonial official in the Western Sahara, Lieutenant Colonel Luis Rodriguez de Viguri, said later that it was US pressure on

Spain which had forced it to accept Morocco's annexation of their former colony.

Behind the scenes in the UN Security Council, too, the US worked to soften condemnation of Morocco's takeover of the former Spanish colony. And in the General Assembly the US abstained on an Algerian resolution which restated the UN call for a referendum in the territory. Morocco, in a foretaste of the diplomatic skills which would successfully confuse the Western Sahara issue in every international forum for a decade, worded a rival resolution which the US backed.

Thousands of Saharouis fled into Algeria from the Western Sahara under Moroccan bombardment of their tent settlements with napalm. The Polisario Front, a student-led independence movement backed by Algeria and Libya, launched a modest guerrilla war for independence of the Sahara against the occupying Moroccan army. It turned into an expensive stalemate over a decade as the Polisario guerrillas developed into a sizeable conventional army with a steadily mounting commitment from Algeria to keep up the flow of arms. Morocco's external debt rose from $2 billion in 1976 to $13 billion after ten years of war. The United States played the crucial role of military adviser and principal arms supplier and equipped Morocco with such expensive and unlikely material for a guerrilla war as F5E fighter bombers and US tanks.

In a great open-air barracks enclosure in the empty stony desert of the unmarked Algerian, Moroccan, Mauretanian and Western Sahara borders, captured US equipment is mute testimony to the depth of Washington's involvement in this distant conflict which, on the face of it, has little to justify a superpower's arms. The clue to America's real commitment lies in the same war museum: neatly lined up on the greyish sand are great rusty armoured cars with their markings scraped off, except on the shock absorbers, which Polisario mechanics dismantled to find 'Made in South Africa' clearly stamped on them in English and Afrikaans. The connection between King Hassan of Morocco and South Africa's ally, Jonas Savimbi of UNITA, is an important one to both of them, but to the US it is a vital piece in their covert African network.

The importance of the network is underlined by the fact that

US intelligence alerted King Hassan twice or more to impending coup attempts by his own top military men. In at least one case the primary issue behind the planned coup was the commanders' wish to sue for peace in the Sahara. None of the coup-planners lived to tell their tale. Later, even the King began to look for a face-saving way out after a series of terrible defeats in 1978, in which the Moroccans sustained hundreds of casualties and whole convoys of vehicles were captured by the guerrillas. Secret meetings were held in Bamako between Moroccan and Polisario envoys in search of a compromise formula which could end the fighting. The newly elected Reagan administration, however, aborted this possibility of a peaceful solution by huge deliveries of US arms to King Hassan. (It was the same technique used by another US administration to ensure Savimbi kept fighting after 1975.) With the ground battles unwinnable, US technology and military aid, with a discreet input from Israeli military advisers, came up with a programme that guaranteed the continuation of the war and imprisoned King Hassan as a client of the US military hardware manufacturers for the foreseeable future. (It also meant that Algeria, as Polisario's backers, would be committed to a continuous drain of resources away from its socialist development programmes.) The US and Israeli advisers threw up a heavily fortified 2,000-kilometre series of six walls enclosing almost the whole of the Western Sahara against Polisario fighters. Advanced radar and minefields needed perpetual servicing by US personnel. America thus began to replace France as Morocco's primary supplier of military equipment. King Hassan put an army of 120,000 men into the Western Sahara behind the wall, along with 100,000 settlers and the Club Méditerranée, with tourists from France and the United States. The latter, in the memorable phrase of a Saharoui official, was, to this austere Muslim society, 'equivalent to installing a Turkish belly dancer next to the Vatican'.

In early 1973 Mustafa El Ouali, the young Saharoui student who was the first leader of the Polisario independence movement visited Tripoli just before the Front was formed. 'We came to Libya barefoot, we left armed', he said later. Gaddafy's support for Polisario preceded that of the more cautious Algerians. From Libya, radio broadcasts, diplomatic facilities and some arms were made available to the student leadership. One of the most surprisingly successful of liberation movements in Africa was led by this tough, highly educated band of men. Over the remarkable few weeks of Algeria's commitment to their cause they had seemingly all acquired the same stamp of moral authority and confidence as was always exuded by El Ouali himself. By then he had died leading a raid on the Mauretanian capital Nouakchott in 1976. Algerian input in training and equipment rapidly dwarfed the Libyan contribution, but Libya retained a high profile in supporting Polisario internationally for the first few years.

In 1976, at the OAU annual meeting in Mauritius, the independent Saharan Arab Democratic Republic was recognized by a large majority at the Ministers' meeting preceding the summit. However, Morocco's threat to leave the OAU if the new republic were admitted to the organization persuaded the heads of state, anxious to maintain the cohesion of the organization, to postpone a decison on recognizing the new state. Morocco's friends, such as Sudan, Senegal and Kenya, also influential allies of the US, did everything possible to combat the Algerian and Libyan diplomatic campaign throughout Africa in favour of Polisario's independence demand. Throughout the next three years OAU missions flew between Rabat and the Polisario's camouflaged bunker headquarters in the border area outside the Algerian town of Tindouf seeking a compromise. They finally agreed to call for a ceasefire between Morocco and Polisario to precede a UN supervised referendum on the future of the territory. By the time of the OAU summit in Freetown, Sierra Leone, in 1980, a slim majority of the heads of state had recognized the SADR and voted for its admission to the continental organization. But still Morocco and its allies managed by diplomatic manoeuvring, clever working of resolutions, press distortion, and pay-offs, to buy time. However the time was in favour of Polisario, with its increasingly professional army and strong sense of nationalism, not the King of Morocco.

The next step towards a diplomatic denouement came in

February 1982 after an extraordinary piece of procrastination organized for Morocco in the name of President Daniel Arap Moi of Kenya, chairman of the OAU. President Moi by then had a sizeable new US military aid mission in Kenya and had given the Americans secret military facilities at Mombasa. As OAU Chairman, Moi announced that the OAU committee trying to organize the peace plan's ceasefire and referendum could not 'name the warring parties'. Clearly this meant that no ceasefire or referendum could be arranged and all the OAU's careful diplomacy of many months was wasted. Moroccan diplomats in Nairobi were jubilant and boasted openly that Polisario's diplomatic status could not recover from this snub.

However, within a fortnight the snub had been reversed when, in the great OAU conference hall in Addis Ababa, the grey-haired, robed figure of Hakim Brahim, the SADR's then foreign minister, walked into the annual ministerial meeting at the invitation of OAU Secretary-General Edem Kodjo. To the astonishment of most delegations the Secretary-General had cut through the layers of confusion around the issue and ruled that the bare majority of recognitions of the SADR was enough to admit the state to the OAU as its fifty-first member. There was immediate pandemonium in the hall as the huge Moroccan delegation stormed out, calling an impromptu press conference on the stairway. The chaos increased as other delegations left the room, and the meeting was adjourned as ministers scrambled for telephones to consult their capitals.

The final total for the walkout in sympathy with Morocco was eighteen delegations, which meant that no OAU conference could then attain the necessary two-thirds quorum to hold a valid meeting under the constitution. For months technical OAU meetings involving ministers in such areas as information and labour relations were bedevilled by airport dramas as one group or another successfully organized the arrival of rival delegations to block a quorum. The OAU was thus rendered completely ineffective. This suited Morocco and its backers because it offered a reprieve from the prospect of an OAU-backed ceasefire being imposed on Morocco, and an implict recognition of Polisario as the warring party, rather

44

than Algeria as Morocco liked to pretend. Such a recognition by the international community through the OAU and the United Nations, would have, as in the case of SWAPO, the liberation movement in Namibia, inevitably confirmed Polisario's legitimacy as the new country's representative.

Worse was to follow as the Libyan factor came to the fore. The next OAU summit, in August 1982, was to be held in Tripoli. The US involvement in persuading its allies to stay away and prevent a quorum was leaked even by several of its best African friends. An American secret document circulated to heads of state was a direct interference in African affairs. It said that the US would not work with Colonel Gaddafy as OAU chairman and further recommended that the SADR be dropped as an OAU member. Even when Polisario offered to withdraw voluntarily from the summit, though not from the OAU ministerial meeting, the Moroccan group refused to attend and so prevented a quorum.

A second attempt to hold a summit in Tripoli was made in November. This one failed too, but by then the SADR was not the only point of contention. SADR voluntarily stayed away in order to break the two-bloc paralysis. But the US took a higher profile than ever in maintaining the split. Its allies, Sudan, Egypt and Somalia, all refused to attend a Libyan-hosted summit, and, at the opening ceremony, a quorum was prevented as fourteen more states walked out over the Libyan refusal to admit a Chadian delegation from the new Hissene Habre government in Ndjamena.

In 1974 Hissene Habre became a household name in France after he kidnapped a French ethnologist, Françoise Claustre, and held her hostage in the Tibesti mountains where he was running a group known as Frolinat practising low-level insurgency. The following year he ordered the execution of the French major, Pierre Galopin, who had come to Chad to negotiate the release of Madame Claustre.

Over the next six years, as governments rose and fell in Chad, Habre was for a time Defence Minister within a Front government headed by Goukouni Oueddei before becoming a self-proclaimed rebel in exile in Sudan supported by the US. Habre was then installed in power in Ndjamena in June 1982 to replace President Goukouni Oueddei's Front government. He came in with CIA military aid brought over the Sudanese border with substantial Saudi Arabian funding, and in defiance of a 3,000-man OAU peace-keeping force. The OAU force had been brought in by President Goukouni to replace Libyan troops which had previously supported the Front governments' efforts to keep domestic order after a decade of factional war. During December 1980 a revolt against Goukouni's Front government by his own Defence Minister Habre was crushed by the Libyan troops. His government's request to the Libyans to leave afterwards was, Goukouni said in a reflective evening in a Libyan hotel several years later, 'the greatest political mistake I could have made'. He said then that his mistake had been in believing that the French were sincere in their protestations of the neutrality of the OAU force. Zaïre was the first country to put in troops and they were far from being neutral, much less willing to safeguard the Chadian central government of Goukouni. The OAU force was humiliated and its impotence derided by Habre's easy return to Ndjamena at the head of a motorized column from over the Sudanese border. Goukouni fled into exile in Libya, via Algeria.

The key to this rapid change of fortunes in the musical chairs of Chadian post-independence politics was that America had been funneling aid to Habre in the form of cash, armaments and vehicles through Cairo and Khartoum throughout 1981. The Reagan administration's veiled and, later, open intervention in Chad appears to have been motivated mainly by its already pathological anti-Gaddafy feelings. (By 1984 the CIA was ready to go as far as involvement in an attack on the Colonel's barracks headquarters during an attempted coup in May, while in April of the following year the US went even further beyond the bounds of international norms with bombing attacks on Tripoli and other Libyan towns.) Chad's near disintegration as a state, the continued factional fighting, death, disease and refugees, inevitable under a weak minority Habre government, did not concern Washington. As in broken Lebanon the US impact on Chad was the destruction of an independent state.

(The French socialist President François Mitterrand, however, initially opposed the US backing of Habre and sought to strengthen Goukouni's broad government by an OAU force which could free him from dependence on Libya and allow the rebuilding of an independent nation. Later, however, French government policy fell in completely behind the US.)

The arrival then of a Habre delegation to represent Chad at the 1982 Tripoli OAU summit was a calculated insult to the organization and in particular to Libya. There was never a chance of it being accepted, but its disruptive impact on the OAU and the Libya-baiting involved was the clear motive of Habre's US advisers.

After a third unsuccessful attempt to hold the summit, this time in the less highly charged political atmosphere of the OAU headquarters in Addis Ababa, a fourth attempt, in Ethiopia and with Polisario again voluntarily staying away, was successful in mid-1983.

Morocco's power to paralyse the OAU by preventing the quorum for so long was mainly due to the unusually heavy diplomatic work put in by the US in this period. A unified OAU ready to press common economic and political demands would have been too great a threat to US interests. Besides, the trusted ally Morocco needed help. Morocco's own diplomatic capacity was at a low ebb, not having recovered from a full year of being completely isolated in the Arab world. During 1977–8 the Arab world's united stand against Israel was broken. This had long been a primary goal of US foreign policy and Morocco's importance to the US in achieving it was enormous. King Hassan was the Americans' go-between for President Sadat of Egypt's contacts with the Israelis, which led to the Camp David Accords. Even Saudi Arabia suspended aid to Morocco in early 1978. Polisario's diplomatic standing in the Arab world benefited from this temporary Moroccan isolation from its brother states, which had repercussions too in fora such as the Non-Aligned Movement and the United Nations.

So, by the early 1980s, the OAU and America's African allies were all that stood between the King and complete international isolation, which reinforced the opposition to him at home fed by the soaring costs of the Saharan war. The threat of the King's humiliation at the hands of his own military was real. But King Hassan's importance to the US on other fronts in Africa was too great to risk his possible loss in a coup. Hence the extent of US diplomatic exertions to mask his isolation and buy some time while, in parallel, US efforts also went into unsuccessful attempts to woo the Algerian government into scaling down their support for Polisario.

Morocco's use to the United States was not only in the diplomatic field as a go-between. In March 1977 a few thousand lightly armed Zaïrean exiled insurgents based on Angola invaded the province of Shaba in Southern Zaïre. President Mobutu's troops could not contain them and within hours were boosted by an airlift of Moroccan troops with French officers and US weapons. They put an end to the insurgency after twelve weeks of fighting. Again, in May 1978, the Katangese crossed the border into Shaba and this time attacked and held the mining town of Kolwezi. After a week they were driven out by an airlifted mixed force which included units from the most trusted allies of the US in Africa, Morocco, Senegal and Egypt. French and Belgian paratroop units also participated.

The two Shaba incidents sealed Mobutu's dependence on the Americans for the organization of the physical defence of his regime. The success of the US-funded military consortium was particularly critical because it reversed a trend in the immediately preceding years when Mobutu had unexpectedly distanced himself from his traditional intimacy with Washington. The US involvement in the murder of the nationalist leader Patrice Lumumba, support for Mobutu's 1965 coup, and the supply of C130s and even personnel for the suppression of the mutinied mercenary and former Katanga gendarme units, had left Mobutu tarnished with US client status. But at the UN in October 1973, in a speech which started a movement across the continent, Mobutu staggered the Americans by announcing a break in diplomatic relations with Israel. For fifteen months US–Zaïre relations worsened, with Zaïre internally promoting a kind of radical nationalism, mostly by proclamation but also by seizing some foreign assets. Mobutu personally, in a public seminar at the African American Institute, accused Assistant Secretary of State Nathaniel Davis of being an agent of destabilization. The Head of State went on to force the withdrawal of US ambassador Deane Hinton (later to be ambassador in El Salvador and Pakistan). His anti-American tirades culminated with an accusation in June 1975 that the CIA was planning a coup against him, and his assassination.

However, the Zaïrean economy was, simultaneously, close to bankruptcy and Mobutu was obliged to accept an IMF agreement before the country's debts could be rescheduled. With none of the obvious reluctance of the Tanzanian or Ghanaian governments a decade later, he unpicked all the Zaïrianization and radicalization measures he had implemented so recently. At the same time, in the summer of 1975, his return to complicity with the Americans was apparent as he began to believe in the possible threat of a communist government led by the MPLA on his southern border in Angola. Mobutu, like President Jomo Kenyatta of Kenya, had been deeply involved in the attempted US brokerage of a tripartite government for post-colonial Angola, which would have been open to continuing US influence through the US-backed FNLA.

Even President Nyerere of Tanzania had tried to persuade Savimbi to settle his old differences with the MPLA and form a unified nationalist government to take over from Portugal. Savimbi received the same advice from the Portuguese left who saw the FNLA and their US patrons, with Zaïre, as promising an uncertain future for the half a million Portuguese in Angola. Savimbi, because of ethnic rivalry with the FNLA's Holden Roberto, was briefly tempted by a tactical pact with the MPLA in 1975. He was easily dissuaded by the US who offered instead to support him militarily. The Americans decided to go for a military solution, as the memoirs of John Stockwell, the chief of the CIA's Angola task force, revealed. First the CIA and then the National Security Council began to fund the pro-Western FNLA and later, UNITA. The FNLA, led by a relation of Mobutu, Holden Roberto, was based in Zaïre, and became the logistics cornerstone of this US operation.

Mobutu, at the behest of the CIA, put his own Zaïrian troops across the border into Angola to link up with the various anti-MPLA forces; these included Portuguese, British and American mercenaries, the FNLA, and regular troops of the South African army. In the chaotic months of Angolan civil war which led up to independence from Portugal in November 1975 liaison was so poor that no clear trend emerged before the MPLA's dramatic last-minute victory. Zaïre had backed the losing side with FNLA. US promises to the South Africans that Washington was committed to backing their invasion with continued military support for the anti-MPLA forces were temporarily stalled by Congress the following month, when the Clark Amendment was passed, prohibiting further US covert aid to Angolan groups.

However, this did not prevent the US administration playing an influential role in dividing the extraordinary OAU summit of January 1976 on the issue of Angola – a precursor of the US-backed paralysis of the organization over Morocco. The US ambassador in Lusaka, Jean Wilkowski, was probably the key influence on Zambian President Kenneth Kaunda in his reluctance to accept the MPLA victory. President Kaunda, like Kenya's Jomo Kenyatta a staunch anti-communist, joined the Kenyan President with a proposal that all foreign troops – meaning the South Africans and the Cubans – should leave Angola and the failed tripartite government be tried again. Kaunda went so far as to say, 'The UNITA–FNLA coalition had every right to request arms from the USA when the MPLA received such arms from the Soviet Union . . . Once Portugal was out of Angola, there was no justification for Soviet support of the MPLA.' President Gerald Ford wrote personally to thirty-two African heads of state pressing for a government of national unity in Angola. President Leopold Senghor of Senegal, another reliable Western ally, not surprisingly produced a resolution for the summit exactly echoing the US theme. President Nyerere said years later that he had intended to speak against the OAU's possible compromise recognition of UNITA, now South Africa's ally, as still a legitimate contestant for power with the MPLA. But he was silenced, he said later, by his close friend Kaunda's open attack on the MPLA for having accepted aid from soviet 'imperialism'.

It was left to the young Nigerian head of state, Brigadier Murtala Mohamed – murdered shortly afterwards in un-explained circumstances – to be the sponsor of OAU recog-nition of the MPLA government. The summit tied with twenty-two votes each side. But the US could not sustain its influence against extensive back-room lobbying, immediately after-wards, by Nigeria, Algeria, Mozambique and Tanzania. The balance changed rapidly because of UNITA's dependence on the South African military, so that a month later, with 41 out of 46 recognitions by Africa's states, the MPLA government became a member of the OAU. Only Zaïre protested openly. And although a diplomatic rapprochement was organized three years later between Mobutu and President Agostinho Neto of Angola, for the next decade and beyond Zaïre remained an important conduit for US and other visitors and equipment for UNITA forces inside Angola.

A Zaïrean, Moroccan, South African and Israeli axis had emerged which was to be crucial for US strategy in a number of African theatres; this included the use of Zaïrean troops to support regimes useful to the US in the Central African Republic in 1979, in Chad in 1983 and in Togo in 1986 after a coup attempt failed, which was blamed on its radical neigh-bours Ghana and Burkina. Israel's significance in this network was discreetly masked. But Israel's own national imperative to divide and paralyse a united Arab front also coincided with perceived US needs, such as that for effective personal security for client heads of state nervous of their own military, as in Liberia or Cameroon. It was also important in the US long-term strategy of ending Israel's diplomatic isolation from Africa where, after a decade, the tide had begun to turn. US allies such as Liberia, Ivory Coast and Sierra Leone re-established relations with Israel. But the axis was most important of all in the long struggle the Americans intended to wage to reverse the victory they had not been able to prevent of the MPLA in Luanda.

In September 1977, just after Shaba 1, Jonas Savimbi was flown by the South Africans from one of their illegal bases in

Namibia to Kinshasa. From Kinshasa he went to several of the African countries which had supported UNITA diplomatically against the MPLA in the run-up to independence. The most important of these trips was to Senegal where the strongly anti-communist francophone President Leopold Senghor had long been a Savimbi supporter. Senghor promised Senegalese passports for UNITA officials. But most important, he was the intermediary between Savimbi and King Hassan of Morocco.

In October that year Savimbi was in Morocco. It was a turning point for the man who had become the Americans' most important player in the Southern African war. Savimbi himself said later, 'I think the meeting between King Hassan and me changed completely the situation of UNITA because King Hassan has conducted our diplomatic struggle. From there UNITA was no longer isolated. The King made his friends our friends.'

Among the King's most important friends were the Saudis who were the main source of the $10 million in cash that Savimbi admitted receiving in the next two years. Later the Saudis would fund the most expensive public relations company available for Savimbi in Washington. In 1986 some of their more concrete support became public when the news leaked of a planeload of weapons for Savimbi, covertly supplied from Jeddah, being flown into Zaïre's Kamina base (see Chapter 9).

Morocco became Savimbi's second home. UNITA headquarters in Rabat were guarded by Moroccan security with all the trappings normally reserved for a head of state. Morocco, where US military and civilian top officials passed regularly as did influential Israeli and Arab delegations, became a focus of American diplomatic activity for Savimbi. From here the training of UNITA officers at the Moroccan base of Benguerir was organized. At least 500 men a year went through a specially devised US/Moroccan course which included, according to Savimbi himself, radio and explosives courses and parachute training as well as basic infantry skills. Arms and equipment from the Americans were also passed through Morocco to Savimbi. Morocco itself sent such items as 10,000 uniforms.

All this was a complement to what the South African military could do for Savimbi to keep him afloat as part of the US gamut of options in Angola. In addition, with the UN arms embargo against South Africa, the Moroccan connection, with the Saudis and Israelis, provided a useful conduit for Pretoria, easing the passage of such equipment as the Stinger missiles, which the Reagan administration authorized for delivery to UNITA in 1986 after the previous year's repeal of the Clark amendment. The repeal, though it paved the way for his visit to Washington and a public meeting with Reagan, was more than just a victory for Savimbi. It was an important marker in the deepening military battle for Southern Africa and was the strongest weapon in Dr Crocker's armoury of initiatives against the MPLA.

So the wide range of US leverage in Africa has been used to divide the continent on the economic and political policies of its own organization, the OAU. The US has also set out to deepen divisions within the political and military leadership of countries as different as Chad, Ghana, Ethiopia and Angola, and between their regimes and some of their Western client neighbours. The weakening of nationalist or socialist regimes within these countries was one of its goals. And all these divisions also served imperialism in its primary aim in Africa: maintaining control of the capitalist state in South Africa itself, with or without the blinkered white regime which was the West's longtime ally.

Chapter 4

Buying time for the West's natural allies

During the decade 1975–85 when most of Southern Africa won political independence from Britain and Portugal, South Africa and its Western allies, particularly Britain and the Unites States, took a long hard look at the region's future. They took fright at the seemingly inexorable progress southwards of nationalist governments with an expressed socialist ideology and organizational patterns. If the trend were to continue successfully from multiracial Zimbabwe, Mozambique and Angola, it meant that South Africa's illegally held colony of Namibia would be next to achieve independence, led by the non-racial nationalists of the South West African People's Organization (SWAPO). Not only would Namibia's fortune of diamonds and uranium then be turned towards the development of the most deprived population on the continent, instead of being exported to the West, but its long border with South Africa would allow armed guerrillas of the African National Congress (ANC) to infiltrate South Africa itself. In different styles Britain and the United States intervened to change the course of this history. Both saw Africa as a porous continent, easily controlled through the Western-educated elite. In Ghana, a decade before, the overthrow of Nkrumah had provided the textbook example of the natural complicity of a civilian and military elite, temporarily denied power by a nationalist leader, with the Western powers. Now, ten years later, Western policy-makers focused their attention on small circles of key individuals who had come to prominence in the independence struggles in Southern Africa.

Britain and the United States were willing to see black leaders come to power in Southern Africa provided that they were neither socialist nor anti-Western. Even South Africa

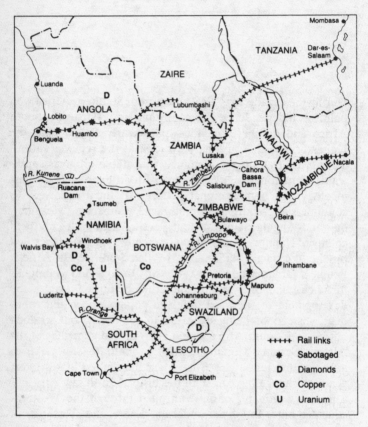

Wealth and communications patterns

was willing to go along with this strategy in the late 1970s, as its abandonment of Ian Smith in Rhodesia demonstrated. But Britain, the United States, and South African government officials have an almost unbroken record of wrong judgements of black African leaders.

From Kenyatta in Kenya, who, according to carefully fostered British propaganda, was the demonic leader of Mau Mau brutalities, to Robert Mugabe in Zimbabwe, described a generation later as a hardline Marxist, British officials saw only what they wanted to see in the colonial possessions of which they were so reluctant to lose control. Like eternal headmasters they tried to perpetuate control through judicious praise or punishment. Nationalist leaders, who sought a real transfer of power and downgrading of Western influence, were either thwarted and eventually murdered, like Patrice Lumumba in the Congo and Murtala Mohammed in Nigeria, or courted with economic privileges until, like Kenyatta, they changed tack. In Kenya, within a decade of independence, Western patterns in the economy and culture were firmly established and buttressed by the constant presence of British soldiers on training missions. The price they extorted was that Kenya deny Mau Mau's history of resistance against Britain and the kind of popular strength and national definition it represented. Kenya, with its white settlers who became influential citizens, its cabinet ministers who dressed like conservative British city bankers, its discreet Israeli and South African links, was the West's prized model for Zimbabwe's independent future. Some far-sighted Westerners even believed it was a model for the distant future of South Africa itself.

Predictably in Zimbabwe at the time of independence such wishful thinking led to Britain's support for a coalition between Joshua Nkomo and Bishop Abel Muzorewa, the West's preferred candidate to lead the rich and strategically important former Rhodesia. They were easily defeated at the polls by Mugabe's ZANU-PF, to the apparent surprise of British intelligence who had worked hard to ensure Mugabe's electoral defeat. Although the new Zimbabwean government under Mr Mugabe practised orthodox economic policies, this was not enough to win unequivocal Western support for his leadership.

Within a few years, South African destabilization, which included equipping dissidents with arms, together with some classic Western media campaigns directed against Mugabe himself, had partially undermined the stability of this important Front-line State. It forced Mugabe into countenancing a degree of repression by his security forces which laid his human rights record open to harsh criticism from the Church, Amnesty International and others. In addition, less than ten years after independence, Zimbabwe had to put 10,000 or more of its own troops into Mozambique against the South African-backed Mozambique National Resistance (MNR) guerrillas, in order to hold open Zimbabwe's oil pipeline and rail route to the sea at Beira. By the mid-1980s the country's own economic development was potentially in jeopardy.

In May 1986 South Africa sent a military unit into the centre of Harare to blow up the office of the African National Congress. Exactly a year later a Zimbabwean woman, married to an ANC cadre, was killed by a South African bomb placed in their apartment. A few weeks later a car bomb ripped through a shopping centre in Harare nearly killing the Brickhills, a white couple active in anti-apartheid work. These were symbolic warnings of how vulnerable Harare's prosperous city centre was to a military power many times more powerful than the Zimbabwean army. They were also a demonstration of South Africa's confidence that its outrageous disregard for international norms, as expressed by unprovoked attacks on its neighbours, would not seriously jeopardize relations with the Reagan administration or with Mrs Thatcher.

Mugabe's government prized its independent, non-aligned status and repeatedly confirmed it by gestures of principle, such as a vote in the United Nations condemning the United States for its invasion of the Caribbean island of Grenada in October 1983. The United States then promptly cut aid to his country, exerting open pressure to conform which incensed Zimbabwe. Criticism of the US in Zimbabwean officials' speeches followed by US retaliation was repeated in see-sawing US–Zimbabwean relations in the mid-1980s, as US officials sought influence over, and even control of, attitudes and policies.

During the Non-Aligned Movement summit in Harare in August 1986, the Reagan administration abruptly announced it would withhold $13.5 million in proposed aid for Zimbabwe after Mugabe, in his opening speech as the Non-Aligned Movement's new chairman, criticized US policies in Southern Africa and Central America, where military supplies to dissidents in Angola and Nicaragua had recently been increased. The aid cuts had been set in motion in July after a similar speech by Foreign Minister Witness Mangwendwa had so infuriated former President Jimmy Carter that he walked out of an Independence Day reception. But the timing of the announcement during the NAM summit was clearly deliberate – a warning to the 101 states gathered in Harare that criticism of US policies could be expensive. To underline the point the US made sure its allies, such as the leaders of Kenya, Zaïre, Morocco, Cameroon, Malawi, did not attend. Such incidents, small in themselves, but cumulative in their impact, illustrate the Reagan administration's readiness to bully Third World countries using economic as well as diplomatic pressures. They go some way towards explaining the gulf of mistrust between most of them and the United States, which has widened into a chasm during the years of the Reagan administration. Southern Africa's Front-line States emerged in the early 1980s as a target of US coercion. Each country in the region was, however, dealt with individually and with a different emphasis. The US coercion of Zimbabwe was just one of the Western methods of weakening the Front-line States' attempts at joint decision-making and action, both economically, through the nine-nation South Africa Development Co-ordinating Conference (SADCC), and militarily.

Western pressures on the Front-line States to reduce their militant nationalism went hand in hand with South Africa's strategy. Though they would never admit it publicly, the United States and Britain were effectively, with Pretoria, trying to create what amounted to Bantustans throughout Southern Africa. Their goal was to have states with black leaders but no real power to control events in their own countries, let alone beyond them.

South Africa, as Prime Minister John Vorster put it as early as 1974, would be the economic and political centre of a 'constellation of states'. Unlike the Bantustans, South Africa would remain safely under white political control. Black leaders would be given no political power. The strategy was to soften the edges of apartheid and pretend that the system of minority rule was being reformed. Meanwhile, every effort would be made, as elsewhere in Southern Africa, to weaken the unity of African nationalism, and discredit socialist aspirations.

By 1980 the United States had 300 companies operating in the country with $15 billion worth of investment. About three quarters of US investments in the continent were in South Africa, and with an estimated return on investment of 15 per cent, compared with 10 per cent at home, US businessmen were initially reluctant even to think of pulling out of South Africa. But, for the long term, America's own racial strains and their effects on domestic politics meant that South Africa and apartheid were bound to become an issue in US internal politics. As early as 1976 the first US buffer against an intolerable future of conflict and destruction in South Africa went up when the Reverend Leon Sullivan drafted a code of conduct for US business operating in the country. The 186 American companies which signed the code introduced non-segregation in their work places, canteens and toilets. Training programmes for blacks were introduced and equal pay promised for equal work. The number of blacks in management or supervisory roles was increased sharply and improved housing, schooling, transport and health facilities were organized. The perspectives were those of America's own 1960s civil rights movement in the South. Leon Sullivan was a black member of General Motors' Board and, through him, the company became one of the most influential sources of pressure for changing the rules and somewhat modifying apartheid.

Neither Washington nor Pretoria accepted the pressure willingly, but over the next few years their attitudes evolved with remarkable speed towards accepting that apartheid would have to be adapted if economic stability were to be maintained. During 1986, a watershed year for the remarkable growth of resistance to the government within South Africa's townships, the West changed tactics and sought a 'moderate' black leadership. Using the Rhodesian model, Chief Gatsha Buthelezi was an early choice for the role of Bishop Muzorewa. But, hedging their bets, South African businessmen and a wide gamut of Western leaders even wanted to talk to the exiled ANC as well. Scholarships, air tickets, funds for all kinds of projects were on offer to the ANC in return for abandoning their armed struggle against the white regime. As in Zimbabwe's bush war, the unrest in the black townships of South Africa had put prosperity at stake.

Pretoria and its Western allies had always believed South Africa's natural future role was to service the vast potential market of the southern section of the continent, a population of 60 million people beyond the borders of South Africa itself. The region's gross domestic product of about $22 billion was operating at a low level of its potential and could be expanded significantly with South African technical input and, of course, with peace. Meanwhile the high capitalization of South African industry acted as a magnet to the unemployed or underemployed men of the region. In a vicious circle, because of dropping agricultural production due to drought and war in the region, men were increasingly drawn off the land to supplement their family income. The old colonial pattern of the use of Africans as a labour reserve was given a new lease of life. The impoverishment of rural areas grew apace as the men left. This migrant labour – about 300,000 men – was a haemorrhage in the economic strength of the newly independent countries and also a convenient buffer for South Africa's industrial barons against their own workers' demands for improved working conditions. Particularly in the gold mines of South Africa, where half the jobs were held by migrants, significant strikes were brutally aborted by the threat of starvation or deportation – which might amount to the same thing.

But the key to South Africa's regional economic dominance is transport. Zambia, Mozambique, Lesotho, Botswana, Malawi, Swaziland and Zimbabwe are dependent on South African-controlled railways and ports for a large share of their imports and exports. Lesotho's entire foreign trade goes through South Africa; Zimbabwe is dependent on Pretoria for 85 per cent of its trade; Malawi is dependent for one third. SADCC, the economic organization for the nine countries in the region, was supported by the EEC and the Scandinavian countries in its attempt to strengthen those transport systems which offered alternatives to South African routes. For some these were short-term alternatives, for the period of pressure on Pretoria and sanctions, but they were also a long-term investment for South Africa if Pretoria could win its battle to become the economic and political heart of the region.

From 1975 and the independence of the two former Portuguese colonies the United States began covertly to back the South African government's increasingly active policy of domination of the region and the 'total strategy' for achieving this end. The economic dependence on South Africa of neighbouring states was seen by the South Africans as one of the strongest cards they held. As one of South Africa's leading academic writers on foreign policy, Deon Geldenhuys, put it,

> Existing economic ties with states in the region should be maintained and indeed strengthened. An obvious precondition for the *strategic application of economic relations* [my italics] is that these links have to exist in a meaningful way . . . The stronger the economic ties with South Africa, perhaps the lesser the chance of their supporting sanctions. Black states could, in other words, shield South Africa from mandatory economic sanctions.*

Through the 1980s the struggle sharpened between this South African economic political strategy outlined by Geldenhuys, and the attempt to build up the nine-nation economic grouping SADCC, as a counter-weight to South African control

*From D. Geldenhuys, 'Some Strategic Implications of Regional Economic Relations for the Republic of South Africa', ISSUP Strategic Review January 1981, quoted in Rob Davis and Dan O'Meara, *Journal of Southern African Studies*, Vol. 11, No. 2, April 1985.

in transport, energy and other aspects of regional economic infrastructure. The Front-line States grew weaker in large part because of South Africa's undeclared economic and military sanctions against them which slowed or closed road and rail traffic. The Front-line States' Presidents' appeal to the rest of the world to squeeze South Africa with mandatory comprehensive economic sanctions was cynically distorted, particularly by the governments of Britain and West Germany; they used the excuse either that the Front-line States themselves were not applying sanctions, or that the black community in South Africa would be the losers.

In the government in Pretoria the defensive laager mentality partly disappeared with the advent of the Reagan administration, particularly with the appointment of Dr Chester Crocker as Under-Secretary for African affairs. Dr Crocker was an academic best-known for an article he wrote in late 1980 in the prestigious US magazine *Foreign Affairs*. In it he outlined the concept of 'constructive engagement' which was to be the main plank of all US Southern African regional policy under President Reagan.

Constructive engagement was designed to end South Africa's isolation from the world community and bring this important US ally back on to the international stage. There was an additional domestic US interest behind the initiative too. Dr Crocker had calculated, ahead of the State Department bureaucrats, that apartheid and South Africa's repression of its black community would soon become a real political issue in the United States. In the article Dr Crocker set out the theory of constructive engagement as a technique to bring the white government of South Africa towards enough reform of apartheid to defuse the swelling anger among disenfranchised blacks. The tone of the article made it clear whose views Dr Crocker found sympathetic:

The way the white leadership plays its cards will help to shape the question of who sits at the future bargaining tables and under what circumstances. The governing white minority cannot solve the domestic political conflict unilaterally. But it could move to defuse a potential crisis, and take steps that would make genuine bargaining possible . . . Autocratically imposed reform could become part of a process leading at a future stage to compromise and accommodation between freely chosen representatives of all major groups.

Between these pronouncements and 1986, Dr Crocker's assessment of the identity of the major black groups evolved and came to include the ANC, or at least what he believed was its moderate wing, which could be wooed away from the South African Communist Party.

Constructive engagement by the United States was focused at first on internal South African politics. But within a year the focus had changed to mean US constructive engagement in the entire Southern African region. Dr Crocker said in congressional hearings in 1981:

Southern Africa is a region of unquestioned importance to US and Western economic progress and warrants a substantial effort on our part to reinforce these prospects and to forestall heightened conflict and polarization. Second, this region has the tragic potential to become a magnet for internationalized conflict and a cockpit of East–West tension. It contains an explosive combination of forces – Soviet–Cuban military involvement, African guerrilla operations across and within borders, a politically isolated but militarily strong South Africa. It is imperative that we play our proper role in fostering regional security, countering Soviet influence, and bolstering a climate that makes peaceful change possible.

The 'compromise and accommodation' which had originally referred to South Africa's internal politics thus became a regional policy of constructive engagement.

Dr Crocker did not, of course, remind his listeners of the original cause of the 'Soviet–Cuban military involvement' to which he referred in backing his claim of potential East–West tension, that is CIA funding through Zaïre for FNLA guerrillas from the north, who tried to reach the Angolan capital of

Luanda on the eve of independence in 1975. Cuban troops and, later, Soviet weapons were brought in by the MPLA to stem the first South African invasion of Angola from the south.

Three years after his first exposition of constructive engagement Dr Crocker was still telling Congress that 'our country can be proud of its record in defining an agenda of negotiated change and regional security in Southern Africa'. The hidden agenda included US diplomatic and military support for UNITA to force the MPLA into a coalition government with a different political line; it was not to be revealed until late the following year when the UNITA leader, Jonas Savimbi, paid a high profile visit to President Reagan and came away with promises of military assistance. Hardware worth $10 million, including Stinger missiles, was provided openly to Savimbi in 1986, but Congressional sources cited another $400 million worth of weapons supplied covertly in that year.

Dr Crocker had the advantages and the convenient blindspots of an academic in his dealings with the white South Africans. His chilly patrician air and fluent and confident exposition of his solutions overawed some leaders in the South African government, though probably fewer in the military. The South Africans had, ever since the independence of Zimbabwe under Mr Mugabe's leadership, convinced themselves, and many of their supporters inside the country and out, that they faced a many-faceted attack by world communist forces. Dr Crocker's elaborate scenario of a jigsaw of initiatives on many fronts suited their own 'total strategy' against what they called a communist 'total onslaught'. He gave a boost to the rising gung-ho mood in Pretoria and provided an invaluable intellectual screen behind which the South African regime felt free to pursue, by decidedly unpeaceful means, the internal and regional changes necessary for its survival.

Dr Crocker never appeared to notice that, just as the Sullivan Principles of work-place desegregation were rejected as mere window-dressing by South Africa's workers supposedly to benefit from them, so constructive engagement was rejected by South Africa's black majority, as it was by black

Africa. Quite undeterred, from 1983 onwards, Dr Crocker and his assistant Frank Wisner travelled with extraordinary hubris between the Front-line States, Pretoria and Washington. Constructive engagement became part of Southern Africa's vocabulary and with it America's dominant role in defining the region's future. The US officials spoke frequently and fluently to the press, and to the leaders of each country, of 'cautious optimism' in finding 'peaceful solutions to Southern Africa's problems'. Political reform in South Africa, independence from South Africa for Namibia, and the end of 'civil wars' in Angola and Mozambique were Dr Crocker's declared goals. They were of course the declared goals too of all black Africa, most frequently expressed by the presidents of the Front-line States.

In the early days of constructive engagement there were some African leaders, notably President Samora Machel of Mozambique, who were inclined to give US goodwill the benefit of the doubt. President Jimmy Carter and his UN Ambassador Andrew Young had impressed many in Southern Africa with an apparent readiness to break with the Kissinger style of bullying the newly independent states of the region and of echoing Pretoria's (quite spurious) security concerns. There was a current of thought in the region that, in the interests of stability for US business in Africa and of the black constituency at home, the United States might well be serious about trying to build prosperous black states across Southern Africa with US capital. Mozambique's linguistic and cultural isolation from the anglophone Western powers encouraged the FRELIMO leadership to respond to US and British proposals with less scepticism than did any of the other Front-line States. President Machel even went on an official visit to the United States and, touring cities in the South and mid-West, tried to interest US corporations in capital ventures in Mozambique. But US business never seriously considered the Mozambicans' proposal that their country's security could be guaranteed by the commitment there of Western capital investment, which the South Africans would not dare to sabotage.

With Angola the US took a different tack. After the MPLA

came to power at independence Washington clearly signalled its view that this was temporary by refusing diplomatic ties, and by constantly holding out this recognition as a carrot to be won by negotiations with Savimbi. Relations between the whole region and Washington soured when the Reagan administration introduced a new factor into the regional political arena as part of constructive engagement. Washington demanded the withdrawal of Cuban troops from Angola as a completely new condition for Namibia's independence from South Africa. 'Linkage', as this idea was known, changed the whole diplomatic scenario in South Africa's favour. It gave Pretoria an excuse for not complying with the United Nations Resolution 435, which demanded an end to South Africa's illegal military occupation of the former German colony.

Neither in Washington nor London, however, did officials initially dare openly to justify linkage on the grounds that the Cuban troops constituted any threat to Namibia, much less to South Africa. 'Linkage' was something of an embarrassment to Whitehall: never clearly disavowed, but not openly acceptable. In late 1987, for the first time, Foreign Secretary Geoffrey Howe stated British policy, accepting linkage and demanding the Cuban withdrawal as part of a 'negotiated settlement' brokered by the US. He went even further, in a letter to Bishop Trevor Huddleston, a longtime campaigner against British government support for the apartheid regime, and suggested that the UN should accept linkage too. Such crude duplicity about Namibia's international status had become the hallmark of Western policy by then. Dr Crocker, who had devised linkage, became known in the capitals of the Frontline States as 'the master of contrived duplicity' (the words of Theo-Ben Gurirab, SWAPO's United Nations representative in the early 1980s and later Secretary for Foreign Affairs). Prime Minister Robert Mugabe of Zimbabwe derided linkage as 'blackmail' and suggested that constructive engagement would be better called 'constructive instigation', as it so clearly encouraged the South Africans to threaten their neighbours. US officials, he said in an obvious reference to Dr Crocker, had 'chosen to be opponents of the rest of Africa'.

Mr Mugabe's message could have been heard from the

leadership in almost every capital in Africa. Dr Crocker's astonishing prominence in Washington and the Western media disguised the fact that he no longer had influence among the African leaders of the Front-line States. Behind Dr Crocker's declared aim of regional peace some ugly and far-reaching implications began to appear with the sudden prominence of the Cuban troops issue. Dr Crocker's peace terms for the region meant nothing less than a change of political character, if not of all the faces in the leadership, in Angola and probably therefore also in Mozambique. The two states at independence had called themselves Marxist, and still, after ten years of considerable dilution of the hopes of transition to socialism, enjoyed good and historically important relations with Moscow as well as other socialist states.

In ten years the original balance of regional forces had not changed, as Dr Crocker knew well when he tried to impose withdrawal of the 20,000 Cuban troops in Angola on the Southern Africa agenda. It was tantamount to a demand for the suicide of the MPLA government in Luanda. South Africa had repeatedly demonstrated its readiness to invade Angola, south of the Cuban-manned defence line across the country. In addition, by the early 1980s, even before the direct injection of US weapons, the South African military had built up UNITA as an arm of their regular forces and a serious constant source of destruction and instability of Angola.

That instability, according to Dr Crocker now, was an internal problem which could be solved by 'Angolans sitting down together'. What he meant was something much more dramatic: a coalition government in Luanda which would send home the Cubans, change its socialist option, withdraw support from the ANC and SWAPO. In Mozambique, too, though less openly, Dr Crocker urged FRELIMO towards accommodation with the MNR, although he knew well enough that that guerrilla group, unlike the clearly pro-Western, anti-socialist UNITA, had no more coherence or articulated political programme than the day it was created by the old Rhodesian Special Branch.

Dr Crocker's pretence that these two South African proxy armies had a legitimate place which could be negotiated inside the two nationalist governments underlay all the manoeuvring of constructive engagement. To those concerned, on both sides, it demonstrated the Reagan administration's ruthless preparedness to rewrite history and to fashion, at whatever military cost to the majority in the region, a future dominated by South Africa's economic and political need for stability and markets. The two Southern African liberation movements committed to a different regional future – the ANC and SWAPO – were, like the governments of Angola and Mozambique, to be alternately squeezed and wooed by the West.

Inside the country constructive engagement brought black South Africans some peripheral changes in their social environment, such as the abolition of the pass laws and marriage prohibitions. The black majority which Leon Sullivan and many other US businessmen had tried to tame with economic gains proved no more tractable with Dr Crocker's political carrots. Grand apartheid, with its forced removals and Bantustans, remained the basis of President Botha's political vision, and was still completely rejected by the black majority. The Indian and coloured communities, offered participation in a tri-cameral legislature, rejected the government proposal by simply not going to the polls.

By the mid 1980s, as township after township in South Africa became ungovernable even with the use of the army, the Commonwealth, which had excluded South Africa from its ranks in 1971, made its own attempt at a subtle kind of constructive engagement. A mission of distinguished elder statesmen (the Eminent Persons Group, EPG), travelled to South Africa and the Front-line States. They talked too to the leaders of the exiled ANC, to the Church, and to labour and community organizations within the country opposed to the existing regime. They tried, and failed, to persuade the Botha government to make some concessions to the black majority which might halt the street violence, school boycotts and rent-stoppages, which had reached the proportions, by early 1986, of an undeclared civil war. The EPG wrote a damning report on conditions inside South Africa. They recommended that the South African government talk to imprisoned and exiled ANC leaders, who had impressed them as men of exceptional stature. But the EPG mission, set up at the Commonwealth summit in Nassau in the autumn of 1985, served only to provide another year without biting economic sanctions for the South Africans, who used it to strengthen further their internal economic base for possible economic ostracism.

Throughout the world it could be seen that Britain and the United States had chosen international isolation in order to maintain their alliance with the Pretoria regime and had made common effort to prevent the racist dictatorship collapsing.

Chapter 5

Namibia – a many-sided piece of the jigsaw

As Western attitudes hardened in support of the apartheid regime there was one area which suffered more clear-cut reversals of the hopes of the 1970s than even Angola and Mozambique. The United States and Britain had been resigned then to seeing Namibia become independent. They believed it would be such a weak state that even the socialist aspirations and friendships of the liberation movement, SWAPO, posed no threat in the long term to Western business empires. But with the advent of the Reagan administration the Western strategy changed. Namibia became key to the South African strategy of harassing Angola by invasions, over-flights, infiltration and sabotage. The Reagan administration slowly allied themselves with this policy until, as the climate changed, they came openly to back Pretoria's plans for preserving white rule in Namibia with a handful of pliant black individuals, in order to mask the illegality of their continued rule.

Namibia, the huge underpopulated desert and bush country on the Atlantic Ocean that is South Africa's buffer against Angola was formerly the German colony of South West Africa. From 1884 until 1915 it was a German protectorate. Then, during the First World War, South Africa occupied the territory at the request of the Western Allies. After the war, in the early days of the optimistic internationalism of the League of Nations, South West Africa became a mandated territory under the League to be administered by South Africa. The huge country, three times the size of Britain, and its 1.5 million inhabitants, were then more or less forgotten for decades except by the Western mining companies. These, from the mid-1950s, were discovering its great fortune of

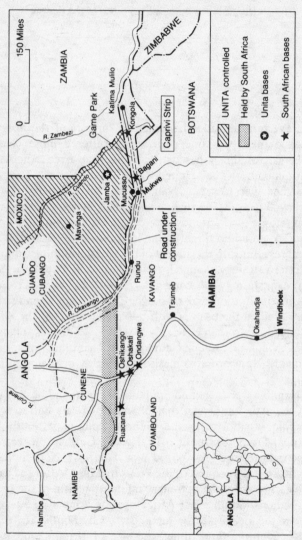

The Namibian border

diamonds, copper, tantalite, coal, iron, lead, cadmium and, most important, uranium. South Africa's then Prime Minister, General Smuts, believed the UN mandate was 'nothing else but annexation', and he told Parliament that it was not necessary actually to annex the territory because 'the mandate . . . gives the Union such complete sovereignty, not only administrative but legislative, that we need not ask for anything more'. This 1920 mandate actually specified that South Africa should not maintain a military presence in Namibia, but General Smuts chose to ignore this.

After the Second World War, however, in a move which would have surprised Smuts, the United Nations ordered South Africa to place Namibia under its trusteeship, a status which envisaged progress towards self-government and recognized the world-wide sweep of independence movements against colonial powers across Africa and Asia.

But South Africa refused then to give up Namibia. It was an early sign of the flagrant disregard for international opinion which would characterize the next thirty years of South Africa's history, as the white government struggled with various political formulae to hold on to power. The cattle herds in the lush northern pastures, and the rich off-shore fishing meant that, with the mining industry (including the largest source of gem diamonds in the world) Namibia was a crucial part of the South African economy. In addition, the territory's actual incorporation into South Africa became politically more and more desirable to Pretoria as change swept Southern Africa in the 1960s and 1970s.

Namibia's nationalists were organized first in the Ovamboland People's Organization, then, from 1960, in the non-racial South West Africa People's Organization (SWAPO). It took them twenty long years to decide to take the same, armed, route to independence as had the Portuguese colonies of Angola, Mozambique and Guinea-Bissau. Only in July 1966 did SWAPO lose some of its faith in the United Nations' capacity to bring peaceful independence, and decide to fight for the independence that Pretoria was clearly determined to prevent. Even so, the organization has maintained a surprising faith in the possibility of diplomatic solutions and has kept diplomatic channels open through a series of serious setbacks on that front. Pretoria's education policy of reserving virtually all resources for whites-only schools had over the years kept Namibia so backward that it was slow to produce a core group of educated leaders with the intellectual conviction to sustain a long military struggle for independence against terrible odds. But the personal commitment of other African leaders such as Ben Bella and Houari Boumedienne of Algeria, and Julius Nyerere, to the old Nkrumah principle that the whole continent must be freed, helped push Namibia's leaders to the decisive refusal of incorporation into South Africa.

Far away from Namibia, on the other side of Africa in the Tanzanian capital Dar Es Salaam the founder and president of SWAPO, Sam Nujoma, arrived on foot through the bush. SWAPO in 1966 announced the decision which brought about a military confrontation with Pretoria. 'We have no alternative but to rise in arms and bring about our own liberation. The supreme test must be faced and we must at once begin to cross the many rivers of blood on our march to freedom.' A month later the first clash between SWAPO's People's Liberation Army of Namibia (PLAN) and the South African military (SADF) took place when PLAN's first guerrilla camp was found by a South African reconnaissance helicopter. The South Africans announced that two PLAN guerrillas were killed. They were the first of 10,000 guerrillas – according to Pretoria's figures – to die fighting the SADF in the next twenty years of a war almost invisible to the international community. Unknown numbers of guerrillas have been captured by South Africans over the years. None has ever been given prisoner-of-war status. The trickle of young Namibians who left the country to train as soldiers turned into a flood after Angola won independence from the Portuguese in 1975. Thousands of people poured over the border into southern Angola or into Zambia or Botswana, clamouring to join SWAPO and fight. Thousands went on to Eastern Europe to return as lightly armed guerrillas who increasingly sabotaged roads, telephone wires and South African military targets in the 'operational zone' of northern Namibia, where the SADF still rules under emergency powers (the Security Districts Proclamation).

More than half Namibia's population lives in the northern area, virtually sealed off from the outside world. Alongside the regular SADF units which permanently and illegally occupy the country, South Africa created the feared Koevoet (crowbar) police counter-insurgency unit. Koevoet has a record for brutal torture and murder of civilians unequalled on the continent, surpassing the much better known atrocities of Amin's Uganda. Over the last decade South Africa has built up a 100,000-man military presence increasingly made up of Namibian nationals conscripted into the South West African Territorial Force (SWATF). SWATF units regularly fight in Angola in joint operations with Savimbi's UNITA. The SADF command structure covers both with their logistics and supply system. One quarter of South Africa's massive defence budget is estimated to be spent in Namibia.

The testimony of Mattheus Shikongo, a young Namibian abducted in Southern Angola in 1986, unusually came to court in Windhoek and his lawyers were able to lift a tiny corner of the blanket of silence covering this cross-border war, fought as much by trickery and deception as by conventional force. Shikongo had been arrested by SADF officers, dressed as SWAPO soldiers and carrying the Soviet-made AK47 rifles used by SWAPO. He was then detained at Ondangwa air force base and later in prison in Windhoek and several times offered freedom if he would work for the SADF. He was even taken to a press conference and asked to denounce SWAPO. He refused and lawyers began a rare court action against his unlawful detention and actually won his release.

Other Namibian court cases have involved SWAPO's PLAN guerrillas captured by SADF or UNITA in the closed military area of northern Namibia or southern Angola. UNITA's Jamba headquarters inside Angola is completely dependent on supply routes through northern Namibia and the Caprivi Strip jutting deep into Zambia.

· Jamba, a show-case village in the bush with traffic lights and other such appurtenances of normality, lies 150 kilometres from the Namibian border. In 1986 the road into southern Angola along the Caprivi Strip began to be tarmacked by the SADF, a clear signal of permanent occupation. A ferry service at Mukwe on the border run by a Johannesburg company, FRAMA Inter-Trading, connects Namibia to another important UNITA base, Mucusso, where there is an airstrip for visitors brought in from South Africa and rough road transport links on to Jamba. And in 1987 a pontoon bridge was thrown over the river to facilitate the major SADF invasion trying to take the town of Cuito Cuanavale. A vast game reserve along the border, closed to the local population of Namibia, houses two major military bases used by SADF and UNITA. The Buffalo base housing the '32 Battalion' of mixed Angolan and other mercenaries, commanded by white SADF officers and used only in Angola, in 1986 celebrated ten years of fighting in independent Angola. UNITA's Secretary General N'Zau Puna attended those ceremonies in Namibia of the unit to which UNITA owed its continuing existence. Meanwhile in Pretoria the UNITA leader, Jonas Savimbi, celebrated with South Africa's Prime Minister Botha his setting up of the tri-cameral parliament, which was intended to ensure the continued existence of the white regime.

Alongside this singularly ill-matched war between SWAPO and South Africa other wars have been waged over the last two decades. One was a diplomatic struggle for legitimacy in the eyes of the international community between South Africa and SWAPO. They spoke for two different Namibias. Much of the terrain for that battle of legitimacy was the United Nations, which backed SWAPO. The future of Namibia was in fact probably one of the factors behind the Reagan administration's campaign against the UN system on so many fronts.

After the US withdrawal from UNESCO in 1984, the Heritage Foundation, the conservative think-tank most influential with the Reagan administration, began to advocate sweeping changes in the UN itself, including a system of weighted voting; this would give the US effective control over the whole organization including the General Assembly, which regularly voted against the US on many issues, including Namibia. These proposals would have changed the international scene in two important theatres where US interests ran counter to world opinion: the Middle East and Southern Africa. International recognition of the rights to independence of Palestinians and Namibians would have been among the first casualties of such a revamped UN voting structure. The US closure of the PLO Washington office and attempted closure of even its UN office in 1987 was a serious diplomatic set-back for the PLO, reflecting the strength of US determination to undermine the liberation movements by all means. The new climate was revealed clearly in public and private meetings in New York, Windhoek and Tel Aviv by Charles Lichtenstein, the US deputy chief delegate at the UN in the early 1980s. Mr Lichtenstein often spoke on South African-backed platforms against SWAPO and alongside and in strong support of those Namibians who had been co-opted into working with South Africa.

From the early 1960s Namibians in SWAPO had received a favourable hearing in the UN for their claim to independence from South Africa. In March 1969 the Security Council declared South Africa's continued occupation of Namibia to be illegal and gave Pretoria the first of a long series of deadlines to vacate the territory; the first date was 4 October 1969. In 1971 the International Court of Justice reinforced the international community's attitude and ruled that South Africa must free the territory. The UN Secretary General Kurt Waldheim even visited Namibia in the following year to underline the need for South Africa to observe UN orders. But it was a vain attempt to impose a UN decision against the wishes, only covert of course, of the major UN powers: Britain, the United States, and the old colonial power in the region, West Germany. As with the history of the UN's involvement in the former Belgian Congo, the West subtly prevented the UN's decision from being effectively carried out. A year later, at the beginning of a series of symbolic gestures which would remain empty words, the UN recognized SWAPO as the 'sole and authentic' representative of the Namibian people. This decision of the General Assembly came under bitter open and covert attack by the Reagan administration officials such as Mr Lichtenstein.

Another UN decision which was systematically ignored by the West during this period was the 1974 Decree No. 1 for the Protection of the Natural Resources of Namibia, passed by the

General Assembly. It forbade extraction, sale or export of Namibia's wealth. But the decree has not stopped vast short-term profiteering by international companies. Rio Tinto Zinc, for instance, have ever since made annual profits of over £25 million partly from the sale of Namibia's uranium. RTZ's Rossing uranium mine in the inhospitable Namib desert about fifty miles from Walvis Bay is estimated to have deposits of around 150,000 tons easily accessible near the surface. It is the largest uranium mine in the world and its profitable lifespan is at least thirty years. Ignoring the UN Decree No. 1, Rossing began mining in 1976, two years after such extraction became illegal. With two other mining companies, Tsumeb and Consolidated Diamond Mines, Rossing dominates the Namibian economy. The mining sector, 80 per cent of which is controlled by these three companies, contributes one-third of the territory's budget revenue. The South African government's policy of buying time to continue its illegal occupation thus serves these international companies equally well. Over forty British companies maintain links in Namibia.

In 1975 and 1976 Henry Kissinger embarked on a programme of shuttle diplomacy in Southern Africa to deflect mounting pressure on the West from African, non-aligned and Scandinavian countries for sanctions against South Africa. Pretoria's devastating invasion of Angola in the run-up to independence had highlighted its dependence on the illegal occupation of Namibia for the logistics capability necessary for that ambitious venture.

To give an appearance of momentum in its South African diplomacy the West devised a Namibia 'contact group', an early version of the later US policy of constructive engagement. The group – the United States, Britain, France, West Germany and Canada – talked about Namibia's route to independence with South Africa and with the Front-line States who put pressure on SWAPO to accept the deal. To all Africans Namibia's independence was a logical expectation as part of the continent's decolonization, but it was also the key to Angola's security from further South African attacks. To the West, granting independence to this weak and disregarded country was a simple way of soothing the growing international indignation against South Africa, and of appeasing the chorus of demands for punitive economic sanctions to force internal political change on the white regime. The independence of Namibia was not even remotely considered a threat to South Africa's own security.

Everyone except Pretoria then believed that an internationally agreed plan for the independence of Africa's last colony would neatly end an historical era. But for South Africa the talks with the contact group were important in making clear that its own long-term agenda on Namibia would in the end be the one which prevailed internationally. In return for its apparent readiness to join the international negotiation Pretoria had managed to extract from the West the concession that both the economically important Walvis Bay fishing and industrial complex and the strategic Caprivi Strip would be excluded from the planned independent territory. Since 1977 Walvis Bay has been annexed to South Africa and administered as part of Cape Province. The talks had shown the South Africans how much muscle they had internationally as allies of the West. The West was apparently content, discreetly of course, also to help in preventing SWAPO, with its foreign socialist connections, from coming to power in Namibia. Indirect talks between the South Africans and SWAPO were initiated in New York with the contact group as the intermediary. But South Africa's Foreign Minister Pik Botha set the tone for the unproductive discussions when he described SWAPO as 'a Marxist terrorist organization' and stormed out. No pressure from the contact group was put on South Africa to adopt a more conciliatory stand, even after the South African bombing on 4 May 1978 of the Kassinga refugee camp run by SWAPO in Angola had killed 600 Namibians. The massacre was clearly intended to destroy the possibility of a negotiated settlement with SWAPO by inciting them to break off talks. (It was in fact a little-noticed preview of some later much publicized bombing by the South Africans in May 1986. Then, with direct hits on three Commonwealth capitals, Harare, Lusaka and Gaberone, South Africa cut short another attempt at negotiations. The Commonwealth Peace Initiative to South Africa known as the Eminent Persons Group failed completely.)

But in spite of Kassinga, SWAPO surprised most observers, and particularly Pretoria, by accepting the contact group's proposals and offering a ceasefire leading towards UN-run elections. South Africa responded, however, by announcing that it would manufacture an 'internal settlement' for the territory with elections in December without UN supervision. The UN, clearly exasperated with Pretoria's stalling, then passed the 29 September 1978 UN Security Council Resolution 435. It called for a ceasefire, the withdrawal of South African troops from the territory and their replacement by a 7,500-man United Nations military force which would oversee elections. A Finnish diplomat, Martti Ahtisaari, who was UN Commissioner for Namibia, became the UN Secretary General's special representative to carry through Resolution 435.

Over the next decade internal settlements organized by South Africa wore various guises. The first was their promotion of the Democratic Turnhalle Alliance, a white Namibian party with a sprinkling of blacks hostile to SWAPO. The DTA controlled Namibia's National Assembly and was increasingly given power and responsibility by Pretoria for Namibia's internal affairs. Defence and foreign affairs remained firmly in South African hands.

With the election of Ronald Reagan Pretoria's margin of manoeuvre in Namibia widened dramatically. In a Geneva meeting of the two sides, organized by the contact group in January 1981, just at the moment of transition from the Carter to the Reagan presidency, SWAPO again offered a ceasefire as the preliminary to implementing 435. Overnight Pretoria hardened its attitude, again refused, and the meeting collapsed. But by the following year, the DTA's President, Peter Kalangula for one had become convinced that when 435 was finally implemented the dependence of the DTA on South Africa would tell against it in the proposed UN-supervised election and that SWAPO would win. Kalangula resigned.

Making the same calculation that South Africa's stalling could not go on for ever, France, with in 1983 a socialist government which included Claude Cheysson as Minister of

Foreign Affairs, resigned from the contact group, saying that it was only serving South Africa's interests by stalling Namibia's independence.

Into the international negotiating vacuum stepped Dr Chester Crocker, US Under-Secretary of State for Africa Affairs. Dr Crocker's constructive engagement policy became the lynchpin of US policy for the whole region. For Namibia the new policy proved a way of taking the issue out of the UN limelight, while the appearance of diplomatic movement bought valuable time for South Africa to step up its military and political organizing against SWAPO in the territory.

Already another component of South Africa's struggle to keep control ensured there were many putative leaders ready to replace Kalangula, and several variations of interim governments available. From the early 1960s Pretoria, alongside its diplomacy, waged a deadly internal campaign of intimidation and attempted co-opting of Namibians, particularly educated ones, into the South African system. The South African-approved authorities in occupied Namibia have done well for themselves under apartheid. An independent Namibia, without SWAPO, could have been the first Bantustan – an example for blacks in South Africa of resignation to an institutionalized future in a second-class country.

Petty apartheid – pass laws, mixed marriage laws, discriminatory property laws – was removed in Namibia in 1981. Nominally, education was made equal for blacks and whites in late 1986, though academic entry qualifications still left apartheid in schools effectively unchanged, because so few blacks could meet the necessary entry standards for decent schools. In the next few years Namibia was increasingly cited in propaganda by South Africa, and by its allies in Washington and the European conservative parties, as an example of what reformed apartheid could mean for South Africa. But at home in war-torn Namibia this South African formula of reform, like the Kwazulu Natal Indaba of Chief Buthelezi often held up as a parallel 'multiracial solution', did not begin to make up to Namibians for the lack of independence from South Africa.

Conditions for Namibia's 110,000 contract workers, often brought from the north to barracks where their families could only live illegally, remained appalling, though South African propaganda claimed that the Sullivan principles of anti-apartheid working conditions were being applied. In the mid-1980s it was estimated that 86 per cent of black workers in the capital, Windhoek, were living below the minimum subsistence level. Single-sex hostels were the normal accommodation in the mines, and fixed-term contracts with no industrial injury compensation gave workers no security. In later 1986 there was a resurgence in Namibia of trade union attempts to win improved conditions. In 1986 two major unions came into being: the Mineworkers' Union of Namibia (MUN) and the Namibian Food and Allied Union (NAFAU). Unemployment, and its inevitable accompaniments of alcoholism, chronic depression, and the sense of powerlessness characteristic of underdeveloped societies, were the background of urban life in Namibia from which these unions grew. Heavy repression and the arrests of union leaders, such as Ben Ulenga of the Miners' Union, was the response of the South African administration.

The statistics of underdevelopment in Namibia are dramatic. Blacks' average income is one-twelfth that of whites, black life expectancy is forty years where white is seventy, black infant mortality is eight times higher than white, one per cent of blacks receive secondary education. Whites receive seventeen times as much of the Gross Domestic Production per person as blacks. In these conditions it is not surprising that Namibia's few schools for blacks became recruiting grounds for South African agents. Traumatic betrayals, splits of the nationalist movement and even deaths followed over the years and contributed too to the holding back of independence.

In 1975, with the collapse of Portuguese rule in Angola, thousands of young Namibians had jumped at the opportunity to join SWAPO in the military and refugee camps of Angola and Zambia. Among them were many infiltrated South African agents, or people who were rapidly bought to become agents. A bitter struggle for power inside the rapidly expanding SWAPO did the organization enormous damage both internally and externally. Behind this power struggle was

South Africa. This period of enormous upheavals and realignments provided fertile ground for infiltration, subversion and the targeting of likely individuals for future roles in the South African scenario of Namibia's future.

The new open alliance of Jonas Savimbi's UNITA movement with South Africa to fight the fledgling MPLA government in Angola meant that old UNITA allies, from the days when Savimbi's was one of the groups seeking independence from the Portuguese, soon wanted to sever relations. (Few knew then what the Portuguese military would later reveal: that before the Lisbon coup Savimbi had enjoyed the co-operation of the PIDE and the Portuguese military to undermine the MPLA's liberation war.) SWAPO, like the governments of Zambia and Tanzania, withdrew from co-operation with UNITA, although communications difficulties in the bush and the inevitable shortages of information, made the cut-off a confused and protracted business. Long-standing personal relations also made disengagement painful and, particularly in Zambia, some officials retained clandestine contacts.

In Zambia itself, amid this confusion in 1976, the SWAPO leadership had to cope with an armed challenge to the authority of its President Sam Nujoma and other key officials. Newcomers from inside Namibia outnumbered existing SWAPO cadres in exile. Overwhelmed by the achievement of independent Angola, the inexperienced newcomers believed that the defeat of the Portuguese had changed the regional possibilities so dramatically that a massive armed struggle could be launched into Namibia from Angola within months. It was a serious miscalculation, partly based on insufficient appreciation of SWAPO's very real shortcomings in experience, numbers and arms, and, more important, the depth of Pretoria's commitment to hold on to the territory. Partly, too, the enthusiasm for instant confrontation was encouraged by apparent new SWAPO recruits later revealed as South African agents – the classic trick of the *agent provocateur* exposing an ill-prepared movement to an unequal trial of strength. South Africa, in response to the MPLA success, was preparing new refinements to a complex plan to maintain political and military control of Namibia and to destroy SWAPO's leadership potential inside the country and out.

The dissidents, as many of the newcomers shortly became, formed a loose group and demanded that a SWAPO Congress be called to elect a new leadership. Andreas Shipanga, SWAPO's publicity secretary long resident in Lusaka, became the focus, or the genesis, of the demand for new leadership to replace Sam Nujoma. At the time it looked to many outsiders like a personal power struggle but, as always with Namibia, South Africa had a leading role in engineering the crisis within the liberation movement. Shipanga would later emerge as the West's favourite candidate for power in South African-funded internal governments (first the Democratic Turnhalle Alliance in 1980, then the Multi-Party Conference of 1985), which embodied every characteristic of South Africa's Bantustans. No one in the SWAPO leadership was surprised by the political evolution of the ambitious, Western-leaning Shipanga. The apparent radical change from the nationalist stance Shipanga had represented when he was a SWAPO spokesman, to his open collaboration with South Africa, was just one public example of how vulnerable underdevelopment makes its elite to being corrupted by power and money.

In co-operation with the Zambian military the SWAPO leadership averted the armed revolt that was threatened by the dissident movement formed on the issue of holding the Congress. That revolt would have plunged Zambia itself into a confused state of military alert, which would have given South Africa a chance to intervene. In the event bloodshed was avoided: the SWAPO dissidents were weakened by being deprived of food and then tricked into giving up. Shipanga and several hundred others were detained, first in Zambia and then, in the case of Shipanga, in Tanzania. It was an act of solidarity by Tanzania with Zambia to house a dissident who otherwise might have been the target of a South African raid to free him.

But in the West the move was interpreted very differently. Shipanga's articulate wife travelled in Western Europe and Scandinavia, and used a network of influential friends in the media and political circles to rouse publicity and sympathy for her husband's case; it was presented as a simple denial of human rights by an undemocratic SWAPO leadership determined to hold on to power by the most ruthless means. In prison Shipanga became a favourite of the liberal press and his detention was used to embarrass and to put pressure on President Julius Nyerere. Criticisms of Shipanga's detention turned into questioning of Nyerere's whole human rights policy. And much of the criticism came from liberal former admirers of Tanzania in the West, who went on from criticism to demands for a liberalization of Nyerere's policies, both internationally and at home, in a wide range of economic and political matters. The 1976 SWAPO detentions of Shipanga and his group of assorted South African agents and manipulable youths saved the nationalist organization from a premature death by Pretoria's embrace. But it sowed the seeds of a Western 'human rights' campaign against SWAPO too. This became an important plank in the US-led Western policy of the Reagan era to prop up South Africa's continued control of the territory. The grandly named International Society for Human Rights sprang up in West Germany in the mid-1980s and became an important source of lightly disguised South African propaganda on Namibia. UN officials and heads of state in Africa were among those bombarded with dubious telexes from Windhoek purporting to be from the families of the 'disappeared' victims of SWAPO.

This confused internal and external battle for credibility led into a second phase of covert internal undermining of the organization. A decade later, in 1986, SWAPO made public the confessions of a number of their cadres, some highly placed, who had been South African spies, often for years. A series of videotaped confessions made against the inappropriately bucolic calm of SWAPO installations in Angola told the story of the effects of underdevelopment from another perspective. There was a striking absence of fear in the faces of those who told these stories on film. Small sums of money, blackmail, threats of retribution against family, flattery, and the perks of office had caught these men and women in the web of betrayal that they recounted. At one point 100 South African collaborators were under arrest. Assassination plots against Nujoma and other leaders, the leaking of plans, analysis and military and diplomatic options to Pretoria over years were revealed in hours of filmed confessions. Among those exposed were four who had even been on the Central Committee. The trauma of these betrayals had repercussions which ran well beyond SWAPO itself and deep into the Angolan armed forces in the south of the country, though Angola never commented on the damage undoubtedly done within its southern command.

But in a move probably unique in the political history of liberation movements, two top SWAPO officials, Hidipo Hamutenya, Information Secretary, and Theo-Ben Gurirab, Foreign Minister, showed the films and answered questions on the whole sordid inside story to invited groups of people in London and Scandinavia in early 1986. It was a calculated gamble to retain credibility in the diplomatic world, where SWAPO had had significant if still incalculable gains against South Africa. The damage was, initially, successfully limited by this openness.

But fear was South Africa's most constant weapon against Namibians. The story of Festus Thomas, tortured for seventy-four days in 1978, was one among many never denied by the South Africans. Thomas was given electric shocks on his genitals, hung off the ground, forced to dig his own grave and lie down in it, made to stand next to a stone being used as a target by a pistol-shooting Sergeant, and held with his head under water until he lost consciousness. A schoolboy, Portius Blasius, was fifteen when, in as random an arrest as that of Festus Thomas, he was seized by soldiers as he sat outside a closed liquor store. Portius was flung into a truck and later beaten as his face was held against its burning exhaust pipe. It takes a brave man or woman to testify to such horrors but many have done so, including men like sixty-three-year-old Ndara Kapitango, who have been roasted on fires by SADF personnel, and women who have been publicly raped by soldiers. A handful of lawyers, doctors and churchpeople have told and retold the stories of South African torture in Namibia, but Pretoria's highly efficient public relations machine has successfully managed to blunt any impact these stories of systematic terror might have had on the international community.

Namibia's own media were severely censored and the one independent church-funded paper, the *Namibian*, was attacked by arson and bombs, its journalists harassed by the courts and their applications for passports often refused.

All journalists have been banned from the operational area of northern Namibia for years except on occasional South African-organized trips to the main SADF base at Oshakati, near the border with Angola. Namibia is effectively hidden beneath a blanket of silence. News from Namibia has been virtually the preserve of a propaganda effort under the direction of Sean Cleary, chief of staff of the South African-appointed administrator general. Namibian offices in Bonn, London, Paris and Washington provided a steady stream of South African analysis and slanted information. This dovetailed with the US administration's effort to portray growing progress and stability in Namibia from constructive engagement, and even, by 1986, a country where apartheid was becoming out-dated.

Predictably, one of the effects of this propaganda campaign was to marginalize SWAPO in much international perception, particularly in the United States. The clear-cut illegality of South Africa's occupation almost dropped off any international agenda. One indication of this came at the Commonwealth summit at Nassau in the Bahamas in 1982. In the many hours of acrimonious debate on the need for common action in imposing economic sanctions on Pretoria the issue of Namibia was allowed to slip away. The mild sanctions finally imposed did not refer to Namibia. When the Commonwealth Eminent Persons Group was formed to explore further what the Commonwealth could do on the question of apartheid, the question of Namibia was left out. It was an omission for which SWAPO was to pay dearly as the Commonwealth became over the next two years one of the most important actors in the unfolding drama of South Africa versus most of the rest of the world. As the Commonwealth and other leaders increasingly met the leaders of the ANC there was a favourable reappraisal of their claim to represent the majority of South Africans. But, while a kind of grudging new respectability was slowly granted to the ANC, SWAPO did not receive any similar reassessment.

SWAPO could barely reach beyond the Non-Aligned Movement and Scandinavia for its international support. But, paradoxically, inside the country, apart from the eleven Bantustan administration leaders who were in the MPC government, SWAPO was getting unprecedented demonstrations of open support. For instance, at a rally in Katatura in July 1986, an estimated 15,000 SWAPO supporters turned out, braving police truncheons and arrests.

Internally the Church has emerged as SWAPO's most important ally and effective leader of resistance to successive South African administrations. The Church has successfully overcome both ethnic and theological differences to provide a unified leadership for Namibians, and what could have been an effective channel for Western political support for change. Only Western aid agencies and church officials in the West tried to keep that channel open. More than 80 per cent of Namibia's population is Christian and belongs to churches which range from Catholic to Methodist. The Churches all have a brave record of denouncing South African atrocities and protecting terrorized and broken people; such as those held for six years in the Mariental detention centre, after being captured during the South African attack on the Kassinga refugee camp in Angola in 1978. As a result of this support for many powerless individuals British, German and Finnish missionaries have been deported, priests have been imprisoned, church services have been disrupted by soldiers menacingly putting guns down on the altar, and many lay officials of church schools or hospitals have been victimized or tortured and detained. Many churchmen are repeatedly refused documents allowing them to travel, and South African churchmen, particularly officials in the United Democratic Front, such as the Reverend Frank Chikane in 1986, are refused permission to travel to Namibia to speak.

Church leaders in Namibia have regularly refuted South African charges that SWAPO is a communist movement. Churchmen, both in SWAPO's refugee camps and in Namibia itself, speak in the conservative tone of most predominantly rural African societies. For instance, Bishop Kleopas

Dumeni, leader of the Evangelical Lutheran Church, refuted the idea of SWAPO as communist in these terms:

> It is propaganda. Who is SWAPO? Let me tell you. SWAPO are members, men and women, daughters and boys of our families, members of our Churches. They are Christians. But the question is why they left the country? Precisely it is because of the hardship of the war situation, apartheid, separate development and injustice.

The tone and the manner of SWAPO's own leaders are similar. Nothing better exemplifies South Africa's attempt and failure to destroy the nationalist movement than their actions against the Secretary General of SWAPO, Andimba Toivo Ja Toivo. Ja Toivo, a former trade unionist, spent sixteen years of prison and torture on Robben Island convicted of 'conspiracy to overthrow South African rule' in Namibia. The logic of this charge meant that the whole of the United Nations should have been there too, for voting for the end of South African rule. In 1984, four years before his sentence was due to end, Ja Toivo was visited in prison by Sean Cleary, South Africa's key official on Namibia; in an initiative which sprang from constructive engagement, Cleary tried to persuade him to leave detention and enter political negotiations with South Africa. Ja Toivo, a gentle, grey-haired giant of a man, explained afterwards the utter misunderstanding that underlay these meetings.

The South Africans and the Americans had, after the Nkomati agreement with Mozambique in March 1984, persuaded themselves that a similar conciliatory pact could be made in Namibia. Mr Cleary, in as famous an article as Dr Crocker's on constructive engagement, had set out his idea that SWAPO's legitimacy could best be destroyed by persuading its leaders to join the internal political groupings preparing for a measure of self-government under the South African-sponsored Multi-Party Conference. Ja Toivo, they believed, would be the ideal bridge between the external SWAPO leadership and the internal parties or he even might be a moderate replacement for Sam Nujoma, SWAPO's President, who had long been supported by Angola, Cuba, the Soviet Union and other socialists.

As Ja Toivo was released from prison, Andreas Shipanga the

once-detained SWAPO dissident allowed to return to Namibia by the South Africans, and an important symbolic figure in the internal party known as SWAPO-Democrats, stepped up to meet him. The elderly Ja Toivo simply turned away. Mr Cleary, a typically blinkered South African official in his dealings with blacks, could not have more completely misunderstood his man and the motivations of the independence movements. But he did not give up without another show of strength. Ja Toivo was refused a passport unless he renounced violence. But the old man instead called for an escalation of the guerrilla struggle. His echo of the external leadership's positions confounded the South Africans. After a while Cleary gave up, and granted the passport, but with a proviso which made it invalid for travel to the United States. However, within months Ja Toivo became one of SWAPO's most effective representatives abroad and one of Southern Africa's clearest voices in condemning US and British regional policy, particularly the linkage of Namibian independence to the issue of the withdrawal of Cuban troops from Angola. According to Toivo 'If ever the Cubans left, the South Africans would have already prepared the next excuse for not implementing the UN Resolution on our independence.'

By the mid-1980s, as the guerrilla war escalated inside northern Namibia and the MPC looked increasingly unable to sustain even the charade of running the country, Namibian whites and business people who had earlier crossed the Orange River to settle in South Africa began to flee the effects of the war of the townships and trickle back into Namibia. Increasingly too they went to Lusaka to meet the exiled leadership of SWAPO, just as South African businessmen went to visit the ANC to gauge the possible shape of the future. But the US administration, more deeply committed to Savimbi than ever, meanwhile started a new round of attempts to trick the MPLA into a tacit agreement with UNITA on reopening the Benguela railway. Behind it lay a disguised sell-out of SWAPO to South Africa, whose allies at the same time redoubled their efforts to delegitimize SWAPO as Namibia's representatives. South Africa and the West, in defiance of the UN, even prepared for the possibility of a UDI in Namibia. But the sweeping military defeat of South Africa at Cuito Cuanavale in southern Angola in March 1988 forced Pretoria to give up that option and grudgingly grant independence.

Chapter 6

Fire-power

_____

1. Huambo – Angola's Central Highlands

Injuries caused by land mines are all the same. Every bed in Huambo hospital has swollen red stumps where arms or legs should be. Every face has the same expression of shocked disbelief or of an agony mocked by aspirin, the only painkiller. Cuban, Soviet, and Angolan doctors operate round the clock or treat skeletal children for malnutrition, without mains electricity, constant running water or sufficient drugs or equipment.

Andrew Young, President Jimmy Carter's United Nations representative, who was much respected in Africa for his honesty and his attempts to press for majority rule in Southern Africa, never actually visited Huambo or even Angola, although even then in the late 1970s Angola was clearly the key to resolving the regional war.

Years later, in 1986, when UNITA's leader Jonas Savimbi was being fêted in Washington by the Reagan administration, Andrew Young and Jimmy Carter visited Ghana and a handful of other African countries to promote better farming practices on the continent racked by drought and famine. It was their way, they said, of keeping in touch with the continent, but it looked more like a safe retreat from the real political issues of Africa.

In the comfortable surroundings of a US official's drawing-room in London, Andrew Young wondered aloud about how much control Savimbi had over Huambo and the countryside of the Central Highlands. He had, apparently, never talked to anyone who had seen firsthand how terror was used by UNITA instead of anything an American congressman would recognize as politics. Young was stunned into silence by the story of

Huambo's hospital. He looked back then on the years when he failed to use his political influence in Washington for Angola. Quietly he said how much he regretted never having fought the powerful hawks in the administration over diplomatic recognition for the MPLA government in Luanda. Deep in too many battles on too many foreign policy fronts he missed the moment when Angola's independence could perhaps have been bolstered against South Africa by the international community's open backing. The US withholding of recognition was just another phase of a war in Southern Africa which very few Americans knew or cared about. Andrew Young, like almost everyone outside Southern Africa, could not then imagine the extent of the destruction Pretoria would be prepared to unleash across the region. But his failure to grasp its significance as a struggle to the death ten years later was due to Brecht's 'blanket of silence' in place again. Andrew Young, in power or out of it, would never have been in control of the web of US covert action in Africa. Nor could he have imagined that in Reagan's Washington there would be such a ruthless commitment to the destruction of the MPLA in Angola and such an open, unashamed participation in carrying it out, as their recognition of UNITA demonstrated.

There is an annexe to the hospital in Huambo which is unbearable to visit. Across the town, with its pretty park filled with new swings and slides, streets shaded by great jacaranda tress dropping blue-purple carpets of flowers, down a track, lies a huddle of small concrete buildings. Outside them sit or lie patients or their relatives. A palpable atmosphere of despair hangs over silent, motionless groups of people traumatized by the collapse of a private world – family, home, farm, blown up or set ablaze. On the concrete floor of the first small room a disfigured child sits quietly against a legless woman who is feeding him. A row of people lie immobile on thin blankets. On a cot with a curtain rigged up to give a little rare privacy a small girl with two limbs amputated has been screaming in pain for two days. No one from her family survived the UNITA attack on her village which took her leg and arm. Her previous identity is wiped out. Her future is too bleak to contemplate in an orphanage here, where international agencies such as UNICEF have made a mockery of their concern for children's dignity. By giving only the minimal aid to keep children alive in well-scrubbed empty rooms devoid of posters, paints or footballs, the international aid agencies fall far short of the grandiose achievements they claim at a distance of thousands of miles away from the war. These too-quiet children will not be a generation of fighters.

There is a poem by one of Angola's finest poets, Costa Andrade, which was written for Paulo Jorge, Angola's former foreign minister. This man, one of the country's best known international spokesmen, for years at the United Nations tried to rouse world interest in the relentless crippling of his nation. The poem, from the first liberation war, could have been written for that little girl in Huambo more than a decade later.

> Those who discuss
> the dimension of bright red
> and write treatises
> on the function of colour
> never saw
> the red of a wound opened
> by the burst of a grenade . . .

Another poem, written in those days when the world preferred not to know what Portugal's conscript soldiers were doing to Angolans could have been written for Andrew Young, who, deep in the bureaucratic wranglings of power, never bothered to see for himself:

> I want to see here
> on this soil stained
> with the blood of a twelve-year-old youngster
> the mothers of the free children
> of the same age.

In the Huambo hospital annexe one Swiss nun with an otherworldly serenity confronts the misery, with no drugs and no running water. A handful of Angolan Red Cross volunteers dress wounds and cook huge casseroles of a kind of gruel which serves to keep the patients alive and no more. The women and children here – there are few men – are brought from the hospital when no more can be done for them there and the beds are needed for the never-ending flow of new emergencies. In ten years of independence this town – once, briefly, claimed by Savimbi as his capital – has never known peace. On every street as people go about their business, to work, to market, to school, trouser legs flap in the wind and the click of crutches on the pavement mingles with footfalls. These are the mine victims of yesterday, last month, last year. Today new amputees arrive daily in the hidden war of attrition against civilians. No one knows exactly how many amputees South Africa (and its allies which provided NATO mines) gave Angola in the first decade of independence.

In 1985 Lucio Lara took personal charge of an attempt to count the amputees nationwide and examine the experience of others, such as Vietnam, to see how best they could be integrated into productive work. Like all Angola's human problems the amputees' numbers and needs were so overwhelming, so far beyond the country's resources, that only the extraordinary courage, compassion and long historical perspective of some of the leaders could have equipped them to tackle the situation. In 1986 the government's estimate was that there were 20,000 such maimed citizens.

One night in the farming country of Malanje province, far to the north of Huambo, there was a party. The tables were covered with overflowing dishes – heaped rice, fried potatoes, bread, greens, cakes, chicken. Women were in their best dresses, children had carefully plaited hair. Lucio Laro was the guest. As the visitors ate, one group of children after another danced, sang, mimed small scenes. At the end a little girl brought him a carefully written letter from the Agostinho Neto Pioneers asking for help to buy musical instruments so that their entertainments could be better for future visitors. 'The very small requests of people who have nothing are hard to receive when you know that our realities mean we cannot meet their faith,' he said quietly as the child turned away. Peasants danced traditional dances of seasons, courtships and harvests and a few old traditional drums and a fine big xylophone were played. Then the music changed. The Cuban school science teacher and his wife sprang on to the floor and two young Angolan schoolmistresses, all high-heels, best dresses and flashing eyes, asked Lucio Lara and his host the Colonel, the highest official in the province, to dance. There was a moment of appreciative silence among the older peasants as Lara rose to dance an old-fashioned waltz. His grave smile and close attention were bent to the young woman's problems of trying to educate scores of children with minimal facilities and equipment for a future whose chances of a recognizable normality were receding with every month's new crop of sabotaged bridges, mined roads and terrorized maimed peasants.

In Huambo hospital's comfortless concrete sheds the majority of the maimed peasants are waiting for a fitting of an artificial limb which gives them a chance to farm again in their village – if UNITA will let them. But, after an attack, UNITA leaves rings of mines in the fields and in the approaches to streams and rivers around the highland villages. Hundreds of young men and boys have been kidnapped or press-ganged into UNITA's ranks during these raids. Going home to grow food again is a bleak and frightening prospect for a woman who may have lost limbs and children simultaneously. Even after government troops have cleared the visible mines the fear can never be expunged. Normal family life has gone for ever for so many peasants of this post-independence genera-tion, and the great hopes of a prosperous peasant culture in this rich countryside have been set back too far for many people's vision to stretch.

Destruction is part of everyday life in the town of Huambo itself too, where UNITA men or their collaborators have frequently been able to enter even the centre of the town, abducting officials, blowing up their cars or homes, and the hotel for visitors from the capital or abroad. Each incident, which even if known in the wider world would appear only as a triumphal paragraph in a press release from UNITA in Lisbon, leaves a community paralysed by fear and thrown back into self-absorption in a smaller and smaller world. When every move is dangerous people's instinct is to stay close to home; organization, the basis of the new life the MPLA promised, is threatened with collapse. In 1984, for instance, in a miraculous

97

escape for the passengers of an Angola Airlines plane, the pilot managed to bring it straight back down on to the tarmac at Huambo after a bomb in the luggage hold exploded on take-off, flinging the torn skins and pulp of a crate of tomatoes among the passengers' legs. Some months later, late on a quiet afternoon on a main street in the town, the Hotel Amirante was shattered by a bomb blast; its walls and windows were blown across the road, as children were going home from school. The noise was audible throughout the town. Distraught mothers raced to the cordoned-off street as rumours of the number of dead tore through offices and neighbourhoods. Personal insecurity haunts every family, every day, every minute.

In a telling symbol of the level of calculated cruelty of UNITA's political tactics they have more than once made an arson attack on Huambo's Bomba Alta centre for making artificial limbs. The morning after one attack the buildings were charred, the raw materials incinerated and the equipment melted beyond recognition by the intense heat. This was professional arson with paraffin or petrol thrown through the windows to ensure thorough burning.

Bomba Alta and even Red Cross personnel have been UNITA targets more than once in the Central Highlands. Foreigners and foreign installations are constant targets of UNITA, as of MNR in Mozambique, because of their high publicity value. The Red Cross, in fact, briefly pulled out of Huambo in the early 1980s after a kidnapping of their staff by UNITA. But, back in action the very morning after the fire, the Red Cross employees started to wash the blackened walls of Bomba Alta before the ashes were cold, and a telex for new supplies went to Geneva headquarters within hours. Even the foreigners who work in Huambo seem to take on some of the heroic stoicism of the town's inhabitants.

The same day, at dusk, in the garden of a large house filled with the smoky scent of jacarandas, the earlier ugly realities faded into the backdrop of an amazing normality. At an affectionate farewell party for one of the Cuban officers who had been part of the people's lives for years, and who had even volunteered for a second tour on the Huambo defence line, cake was passed round, and teenagers danced to the latest cassettes from Portugal and Brazil. The talk was of poetry, plants, the Palestinians and the recent massacres of the Sabra and Chatilla camps – beauty, loss, pain and tenacity encapsulated safely in other experiences. By tacit consensus no one spoke of the death and despair which lurked so close every minute just outside the gate and the warm family circle. The strain which has never eased up, and which only extreme personal and group discipline keeps under control, has marked every face with an ageless unworldliness. Very late, and to a stranger he would never see again, one young man said softly the unsayable, 'I'm not sure how long I can live like this.'

But life goes on as though everyone has learned to forget or transcend its precarious context. At the weekend the football stadium at the edge of the town is packed for a match between two military teams and again the illusion of normal life flowers for a few hours. But even normal pleasures lie paper-thin over everyone's tension. A young soldier's pistol goes off as the goal-keeper on his team lets in the ball, and a frantic scramble ensues as the rumour of 'UNITA' whips through the crowd.

There is an orchid house outside Huambo. It is a poignant illustration of how far people will go to safeguard the beautiful and life-enhancing against the threat of barbarism and cultural desolation. In a long plastic greenhouse great trailing tentacles, bearing the strangely indestructible and perfect brown, purple and pink orchid heads, climb out of mossy baskets or along an old piece of wood. Delicate white begonias, huge ferns and shiny leafed scarlet anthuriums evoke another life where calm reflection, leisure and study could be the norm. Chianga, an experimental agricultural station, part of the university, was bombed and its entry road mined a week before. However, the grass in the citrus orchard is newly trimmed. And normal work continues too in the laboratory of soil samples for the whole country. Thousands of glass sample bottles, miraculously intact after the bomb attack, are neatly dusted and the map of the country being drawn showing the distribution of their contents is creeping slowly towards a finish. Gaping holes in the tarmac road leading into the campus and huge plastic sheets over shattered library walls will be reminders of the attack for the indefinite future. The resources to repair sabotage are simply not available. Even the sabotage of the important Lomaum dam, which cut off water and electricity supplies to the whole province and to Benguela cannot be repaired because of the lack of security. Military resources are spread so wide in this huge country that there is no certainty of being able to prevent another sabotage.

At Chianga South Africa has etched yet another notch in the decline of the country's normal functioning. But the unchanging endurance and stubborn faith which sustained the MPLA through previous phases of war is still alive. The last entry in Chianga's visitors' book, and the first after the attack, was in Lucio Lara's distinctive literary handwriting. He had flown from Luanda for the day to see the damage, and written a paragraph of measured congratulations on Chianga's high standards of academic and scientific work. There is no hint of despair here at the creeping paralysis of independent Angola that has left Huambo like an island cut off from the rest of the country and the rest of the world, except in spirit.

South Africa has for a decade done here with UNITA what Luis Jose Cabaco, one of FRELIMO's key officials, on the other side of the continent once described as 'the unpicking of the social fabric'. MNR in Mozambique, too, has made a deliberate attempt to return peasants to the old world of the uneducated, disorganized and therefore powerless mass that colonialism held in thrall so easily. Mozambique's Prime Minister Mario Da Graca Machungo spoke, ten years after independence, of education as the key to the country's battles 'so that our citizens are no longer circumscribed by their village, but understand that village's place in our nation and Mozambique's place in the wider world'. Men like this, and like Lucio Lara, are intellectuals who have plunged themselves into the strenuous practical work of transforming societies as fragmented and backward as the Soviet Union was during the Bolshevik Revolution. To all of them education is the centrepiece of the post-independence period. In Mozambique, for instance, where 85 per cent of the population was illiterate at the time of independence in 1975, the immediate post-independence effort put into education meant a doubling of the number of teachers and a reduction of illiteracy by one quarter over five years.

2. Inhambane – Mozambique's Indian Ocean Coast

A certain village has been newly created for the lawless bands which are dignified with the description of former guerrillas of the Mozambique National Resistance (MNR). It would take an hour or more to walk to it from the tarmac coast road. The dusty path winds through shoulder-high grass which touches the big scarlet leaves of cashew nut trees, criss-crossing a narrow stream with shaky planks thrown across it. Several times it divides into two paths, and someone must go back to the last low house made of woven sticks under a grass roof to ask directions from a woman cooking over a fire of sticks, or from a band of children intent over a game with stones. Such a road in the cashew forests on the coast of Kenya or Tanzania leads to idyllic white beaches and noisy pink European tourists, or dignified Swahili fishermen living lives little touched by anything beyond the mosque, and occasional visits from the sons who went to prosper in the hustle of offices in the capital. This one leads to the sons and daughters who can never return home because they have spent weeks, months or years in passionless killings aimed at the soul of FRELIMO, the peasants of Mozambique.

A cardboard sign saying 'Stop' is strung across the path on a fraying piece of string. The FRELIMO soldier on guard casually drops the string. There are no formalities when visiting yesterday's enemies. 'People are people, we do not try to keep them like dogs,' said the FRELIMO Major in charge. But no one runs away from here, there is no way back to where they came from.

This village was started in 1984 as FRELIMO attacks on MNR bases began to reveal dozens, then hundreds, then thousands of people who had been with the MNR for no clear reason but were not prepared to fight for them once confronted with a FRELIMO force.

The former guerrillas straggled in from the fields in response to a whistle blown by the FRELIMO commander in charge of the village. Like them he was dressed in old jeans and a T-shirt, but his face set him apart as though he came from another country.

The laughing shining eyes and confident bouncy manner were those of the boy he had been twelve years before, when he turned his back on Portugal's decaying colony and simply walked away over the border. Speaking only Portuguese and with no education he found his way through Zambia to Tanzania and FRELIMO's leadership. One year in Moscow left him with the unshakeable conviction that the world was small and anyone could do anything in it. Such an attitude could hardly be farther from the fatalism inculcated by the Portuguese in their colonies as a method of maintaining domination.

Facing the FRELIMO commanders the village inhabitants, men and women, shut their faces. Each one who spoke told the same short and unconvincingly matter-of-fact story. Remarkably, none tried to avoid the responsibility for the horrors they had committed. No one could explain why they had lived as outlaws wreaking terror on isolated villages and ambushing buses or trucks full of civilians or food. A young woman with broken brown stumps for teeth and a relentless scowl said, through smiling interpreters and in response to a question, that she was happy to be with FRELIMO. But her dull beaten eyes told a different story: days with FRELIMO were no different from other days, the future had no more interest for her than the past, nothing could touch her any more.

Next to her were two boys of thirteen and fourteen. One, describing his past killings and future hopes that his mother might appear and take him home, had a seraphic smile – at second glance the dazzle of the successful conman.

An elderly man stepped forward to explain how he had ambushed fifteen buses and trucks and killed countless people. It was a story he had told many times and he was used to getting a lot of attention for it. He smiled as he told it. And his FRELIMO hosts smiled politely too. Rage, hatred and the desire for retribution are not the style of the authorities here. Instead the FRELIMO commanders take pride in stressing the normal life of the village. The huts laid out in neat rows mirror the pattern of FRELIMO communal villages. Many of the former guerrillas have married, either girls who were in the MNR camps or in some cases local girls whom they met at dances and feast days to which nearby villages, astonishingly, invite them.

The FRELIMO Major, like a mother reminding a child of its manners, asked the villagers to dance, to entertain the visitor as thanks for the long journey. Afterwards, in the footsteps of an energetic security guard checking for mines, there was a tour of the plots of carrots, tomatoes and potatoes, which the vilagers have been taught to raise on an irrigated patch of sandy soil in the shadow of the sand dunes bordering the ocean.

There is no political education here in the style of the early years after independence, when FRELIMO re-education camps fought an aggressive cultural and educational battle against the attitudes bequeathed by Portuguese colonialism. Only the systematic degradation of the African population to a condition unenlightened by such ideas as nationhood or patriotism, or history, and with no future beyond the confines of a village cycle of birth, slave work, death, can explain how South Africa could turn thousands of Mozambicans into its mindless agents of death and destruction over the first decade of independence. The deliberate economic destruction sown by MNR in the countryside rendered the peasants even more vulnerable to the dictates of these outsiders; they had destroyed their modest self-sufficiency and so created a new dependence on food aid from the West, or, for the thousands who stayed with the rebels, supplies brought in for MNR by South African airdrops or even submarine landings.

In the hospital wards of Inhambane, two hours or so away by road, lay evidence of these guerrillas' recent past. Two old white-haired women sat confused, rocking themselves. Both had a characteristic dressing across the back of the head – it had been sliced with a machete. Only Malangatana's paintings can capture the impact of the horror, still naked in these women's eyes, at the tide of terror which engulfs the villages they come from. The horror of the MNR is its unpredictability. It needs no reason to strike. From bed to bed in rural hospitals like this in Mozambique the patients whisper the same story of beatings and slashings with machetes from bandits who burst into huts at random during the night, or fell on groups of women working in the fields or eating together at the end of the day.

In the men's ward in Inhambane one evening were a dozen victims of an ambush on the main road three miles outside the town. The bandits had sprung into the road in the silence of the early morning. They were armed with machine guns and bazookas. The new food aid truck crashed into the high grass of the bank as the first bullets hit the driver. Raking the passengers with bullets they killed another dozen people, either in the truck or by hacking them to pieces as they tried to limp or crawl away. Seconds earlier the truck had been full of busy individuals – a man home on holiday from the mines in South Africa visiting relatives in town, men going to work in the port, women workers from the cashew nut factory in the province capital. In that pretty pink and whitewashed, neatly laid out colonial town, with its fountain and pool outside the Governor's palace, and in the whole district, confidence was shattered and sense of purpose lost. After two days in hospital many of the victims were still too shell-shocked to speak or to consider their future. The gang which attacked them made no attempt to get away with the truck, or even to demand money or goods; destruction was the height of their ambition. As FRELIMO's then Chief of Staff, Colonel-General Sebastiao Mabote, put it, 'This is not a war. We know war. We in FRELIMO fought a guerrilla war where, on principle, we never so much as walked on a peasant's sown land. Our targets were the instruments of oppression; theirs, the bandits', are exactly the reverse, their targets are economic and social development.'

Just how successful the MNR have been in hitting these economic targets in some areas of Mozambique could be gauged by the haggard, naked people who emerged like beings from another century after several years of living under MNR control. Some of the women were wearing green shreds of what had been the South African parachutes used to keep MNR leaders supplied with food and arms. In mid-August 1985, in one of FRELIMO's most significant post-independence battles, a combined Mozambican/Zimbabwean force took the MNR's main base, the Casa Banana in the Gorongoza game park in the centre of the country. The MNR was taken unawares by the attack and fled quickly, making no attempt to defend their headquarters, or even to remove the incriminating written evidence of many months, that documented the base's South African dependence.

Among the many papers recovered were carefully kept diaries of the MNR leaders' visits from key South African civilian and military officials, such as Deputy Information Minister, Louis Nel. Less than a year later Mr Nel was being deferred to by Western journalists in South Africa as he ran the ludicrously misnamed Information Bureau, whose aim was to blur the violence of Pretoria's State of Emergency for the outside world.

Why did a minister and senior military officials in the South African hierarchy go on these bizarre night trips? This is one of the many mysteries surrounding South African rationale for its support for MNR. Visiting MNR inside Mozambique was not only a security risk, but clearly potentially disastrous diplomatically if it were to be discovered at a time when South Africa was pretending to observe the Nkomati non-aggression agreement with Mozambique. (However, details of the Gorongoza documents were revealed, with convenient timing for FRELIMO, when President Samora Machel was in Washington, and made barely a ripple in the US; the administration certainly knew the facts of South African involvement well before.) The visits could hardly have been necessary to allow the South Africans to see for themselves how weak a tool MNR was and what depths of duplicity would have to be sunk to to present it to the outside world as a credible contender for power with FRELIMO. The likely explanation was the South Africans' need for such gestures of confidence, to raise the morale of the MNR leadership and of the South African elite troops running MNR logistics on the ground.

These South African logistics experts could organize thousands of MNR men to materialize out of Malawi. Indeed, in late 1986, South African troops led MNR bands hundreds strong down the river into Zambezia province . . . sacking hospitals, health points, schools, railway lines and administrative structures, driving hordes of terrified peasants ahead of them to the very outskirts of the province capital.

Chapter 7

Destabilization – undermining Southern Africa from within

South Africa's proxy armies in Angola and Mozambique have been a direct means of destabilization. Usually destabilization is covert. Its essence is the weakening, or the destruction, of a regime by an outside agency in such a way that it seems to have happened by a natural internal process.

In Southern Africa destabilization was already in process during the end of Portuguese colonialism and the first years of Zimbabwean independence. But by the mid-1980s some international awareness of just how seriously the region's strength was being sapped grew, with aid agencies and journalists at last devoting time and space to chronicle needless deaths and maiming. Too often these were presented as stemming from civil war, but Pretoria's role as mastermind, logistics expert, arms supplier and sanctuary for terrorists before and after their actions, became increasingly apparent.

Proxy armies of destruction and destabilization, less well known than either UNITA or MNR, were created too by South Africa in other Front-line States. In Lesotho, for instance, the Lesotho Liberation Army began to attack economic targets from 1979 and openly offered to stop operations in return for the expulsion of the ANC. When the government of Chief Jonathan refused to accept South Africa's terms other methods were used to ensure compliance by the mid-1980s. These included a blockade of the landlocked country's borders, which brought the government down, and a campaign of terror against individuals, from church officials to ANC sympathizers, with any suspected anti-South African government views. For Zimbabwe guerrillas were recruited in the Dukwe refugee camp in Botswana, trained in the Transvaal, and infiltrated into the chaos and carnage of the southern province of Matabeleland in 1981. This action began to be called Super-ZAPU after the wing of the nationalist movement led by Joshua Nkomo who, with many of his followers, grew progressively away from the government. Three white military officers, former Rhodesian soldiers, serving in the South African defence force were killed inside Zimbabwe in August 1982, when on a sabotage mission from the Transvaal base area where South Africa's proxy armies were being formed. One telling detail, that one of the white soldiers was dressed in an Angolan army uniform, revealed just how closely interconnected were the various South African wars of Southern Africa.

In their different ways Lesotho and Zimbabwe were to be precursors of how a state such as Mozambique could be simultaneously coerced with guns and starvation and wooed with hopes of development capital. The migrant labour force from these countries is also one of South Africa's strongest means of control, both over neighbouring states who need the foreign exchange, and over the individual lives of the migrant workers. Especially in the case of Mozambique these men have been ruthlessly used as political pawns, being hired and fired from the mines at will, press-ganged into the proxy army as an alternative to starvation or even death, and held in thrall by the terrible bond of outlaws joined by common guilt for the crimes they have committed, often in their own home villages. According to Mozambique's President Joachim Chissano boys not yet in their teens have been coerced into these crimes by the bandit groups.

The origins of the Mozambican National Resistance movement (MNR) are a telling pointer to the interests it was, by the mid-1980s, trained to safeguard. They are a testament too to the far-sightedness and determination of some of those in power in white-ruled Southern Africa at that time.

From 1975 several hundred Mozambicans were recruited and trained in Rhodesia by the Special Branch for operations against the Zimbabwean nationalists based in Mozambique and, incidentally, against the FRELIMO forces fighting the Portuguese for Mozambican independence. The Portuguese military intelligence in Mozambique, confused and cut off from the momentous upheavals in their country's military ranks, wholeheartedly supported the Rhodesian unleashing of semi-trained Mozambicans against FRELIMO, whose success was an embarrassing witness to the decay of the Portuguese empire. Among them were even some Angolan *'flechas'* or deserters, one of the many strands of semi-autonomous Angolan military groups (including the CIA-backed FNLA and UNITA). The Portuguese were able to use these to cause complete political and military confusion in the scramble for power that their departure precipitated in Luanda.

But in Mozambique, in the transition to independence, there was no such scramble between competing groups. Earlier contests for power within FRELIMO had been settled after some vicious anti-white in-fighting among FRELIMO's rear-based cadres in Dar Es Salaam. Black power politics among the US-educated Mozambicans was deliberately fostered by the CIA, acting through university conduits that were later well known. One of the key people in this campaign, which seriously weakened FRELIMO, was Jose Massinga, who would later admit, in 1981, to being a CIA agent. He was far from the only one to use the convenient shield of black power radical philosophy to try to oust from the leadership some of the best educated and most articulate socialist and anti-imperialist figures in nationalist movements across Southern Africa who happened to be white. One of the black power activists in FRELIMO was a black American, Leo Milas, who infiltrated the movement in the 1960s, pretending to be Mozambican. He was unmasked by FRELIMO's founder, the late Dr Eduardo Mondlane, in 1966 and expelled from the organization. Later he worked in Kenya for the United Nations Environment Programme. With Fanuel Mahluza, an early defector from FRELIMO who spent time in both Kenya and South Africa, he remained an important link in the anti-FRELIMO international network. Another former FRELIMO student and one who never left the US after completing his studies, Luis Serapiao, became a Professor at Howard University in Washington and the author of many articles attacking FRELIMO openly for its mixed-race philosophy as well as for its Marxism. By the mid-1980s he was not only active on the seminar and conference circuit in the US, but, emerging as an MNR spokesman was received as such by the State Department in 1987.

At its crudest, this US-fostered current, which would grow rapidly in waves during the 1980s, identified whites with communism and attempted to brand them as poor nationalists allied to external powers, namely the Soviet Union. The South African mass movement was initially split on this issue by the breakaway of the Pan African Congress (PAC) from the African National Congress (ANC). The PAC's ideological grounds of difference became ever more fudged as the years went by, but the racist one, that of excluding whites from the liberation movement, was only too clear. By the mid 1980s, the South African Communist Party's support for the ANC was one of America's most open targets in their attempt to boost 'moderate black leadership' within the ANC and other strands of the opposition to Pretoria.

But for FRELIMO, after the crucial and hard-fought Second Congress in 1968, and after the assassination of its first President Eduardo Mondlane by a Portuguese letterbomb disguised in a book, unity and non-racial leadership were achieved; this left, by independence, virtually no rival grouping inside the country. The handful of FRELIMO military dissidents whom the Rhodesians found malleable for subversion were, on the admission of the Rhodesian Central Intelligence Organization itself, poor quality.

The first leader of this dissident group, called by the Rhodesians MNR or RENAMO, was André Matsangaiza, a FRELIMO fighter from 1972 to 1974 who, after independence in 1975, worked in northern Mozambique at Dondo in the army quartermaster's stores. He was accused before a FRELIMO military tribunal of stealing a Mercedes car and numerous other items from the stores and was sent to a re-education camp, from where he escaped to Rhodesia. Using Matsangaiza as the leadership figure they had been unsuccessful in finding before, the Rhodesians set up a permanent base camp for training at Odzi in Eastern Rhodesia.

The dissidents' number two was Alfonso Dhlakama who, after Matsangaiza's death, became the MNR's leader for a decade. Other spokesmen, who were actually Portuguese citizens, with only tentative links to actions inside Mozambique, came and went in Lisbon and South Africa. The best known of them, Evo Fernandes, a Goan Portuguese, is believed to have worked for the Portuguese secret police as well as for Jorge Jardim, the most powerful colonial businessman in Mozambique. He, like the MNR West European representative, Jorge Correia, was expelled from MNR in the mid-1980s when a black nationalist image was sought for the organization. The Heritage Foundation and other anticommunist propaganda groups in Washington began to adopt MNR in this period and to shape its external profile in the Mozambique Information Office in Washington. This was run by an American named Thomas Schaaf, who had worked in Zimbabwe for the government's Agricultural Extension Service near the Mozambique border, until the Zimbabwean security police became suspicious of him and began to watch him closely. He then returned to Washington.

In the early days the anti-FRELIMO Mozambicans being groomed under Rhodesian tutelage were equipped with Chinese or Eastern bloc weapons and dressed in anonymous olive-green uniforms. The *raison d'être*, as one of the Rhodesian Intelligence officers later described it, was that 'the MNR gave a cover for Rhodesian operations and, from initial intelligence-gathering operations, moved on to getting recruits and then on to the offensive, disrupting road and rail links and making it harder for FRELIMO to support ZANU' (Robert Mugabe's army).

But these military manoeuvres did not last long against the Zimbabwean nationalist forces, and the cover for the Rhodesian sabotage of Mozambique could not last beyond the life of Rhodesia itself. At Lancaster House in December 1979 a new constitution marked the end of the white regime and within four months Robert Mugabe won the election. For MNR it was the abrupt end of an era. Most of the MNR, about 2,000 fighters, were hastily sent across the border out of Zimbabwe and into Mozambique. For Mozambique, then in the euphoria of the nationalists' success over the border and with the prospect of the lifting of the UN sanctions which had been imposed against the illegal Smith regime at a cost of £250 million, the MNR fighters were considered a minor problem.

However, FRELIMO may not have known that a full year earlier South Africa's military intelligence, anticipating the inevitable fall of Smith, had opened relations with MNR. They had supplied some weaponry and, more important, committed themselves to giving MNR a base after the white regime in Rhodesia had gone. With the connivance of the British Foreign Office, South African C130 aircraft took 250 of the MNR men, as well as equipment from the Odzi base in Zimbabwe, to the huge Phalaborwa base in the Eastern Transvaal. Here many of the notoriously anti-nationalist former Rhodesian Selous Scouts and other similar units were about to be housed with the SADF. In this highly militarized area near the Mozambican border MNR was just one of the dissident groups to be trained and housed for future use against South Africa's neighbours and other governments, even as far away as the Seychelles in the Indian Ocean.

Even if FRELIMO had known in detail of South Africa's plans for continuous erosion of Mozambique's economy (by what would later become fashionably termed 'low intensity conflict') the Party could have done little about it then. FRELIMO's handful of overworked cadres were absorbed in the overwhelming problems of trying to cope with the infrastructure sabotaged by the departing Portuguese, with a fragmented country, which FRELIMO had only very partially penetrated before independence, and which spoke thirty-two languages and had no tradition or conception of unity. The social transformation promised by FRELIMO, based on education, health and nationalism, demanded total attention. President Samora Machel's confident assertions that the 'armed bandits' of MNR were no threat predated the ambitious new plans for Mozambique which the South African military began to evolve; this was in response to the new circumstances in the region created by the failure of the pro-Western Bishop Muzorewa in the Zimbabwean elections.

Across the continent independent Angola was giving sanctuary, training and support to SWAPO to step up the war for independence in Namibia with its obvious implications for a guerrilla option within South Africa. Mrs Thatcher, previously convinced by her officials that Bishop Muzorewa was a real candidate to lead a pro-Western Zimbabwe in which the existing white power structure need not be unpicked, changed her mind in forty-eight hours during the Commonwealth summit in Lusaka in August 1979. The viability of the 'internal settlement' could not, she saw, be maintained in the face of united African opposition, most crucially from Nigeria, an important economic partner for Britain. She announced the Lancaster House Conference for later in the year, to be followed by elections in which the Patriotic Front of Robert Mugabe and Joshua Nkomo would participate. But even at this late stage on the road to a real independence for Zimbabwe the British tried by all possible means to cripple the armed wing of the Patriotic Front. Essentially the guerrillas were confined to 'assembly points' during a ceasefire while the white Rhodesian units under General Walls were allowed complete freedom of movement. General Walls said openly during Lancaster House that his forces would fire on the guerrillas during the election if they moved from the assembly points. The ceasefire therefore contained all the elements of a potential massacre of the guerrilla army; thanks only to the brave and consistent behaviour of the Commonwealth Monitoring Force of 1,400 British, Australian, New Zealand, Fijian and Kenyan troops such a disaster was averted.

The Patriotic Front split after Lancaster House. Britain then hoped for a coalition between Joshua Nkomo's ZAPU party and Bishop Muzorewa. Twenty seats were reserved for whites, and Whitehall believed that a weak and unstable coalition would block Mugabe.

But Robert Mugabe's ZANU won the election outright, and a pliable Zimbabwe was clearly no longer available as a model and as a possible black African base for training dissidents for Pretoria's future use in Southern Africa. The West looked elsewhere. Malawi, under the eccentric Dr Hastings Banda, was a reliable friend of the West. At his Kamuzu Banda Academy for the elite of Malawi the President was safeguarding the ideological future of his country. Latin was an obligatory subject, and a succession of British schoolmasters extolled the values of a suburban, conservative England as outdated as colonialism. And authoritarian style was taken further in the Israeli-run Young Pioneers. Malawi would be the base for future phases of South African destabilization, although it would be several years before first Mozambique, then Zimbabwe, revealed the devastating toll of rural destruction caused by Pretoria's proxy armies coming through Malawi.

In Mozambique from 1980 the targets of the 'armed bandits', as the government called MNR, were every aspect of the newly built infrastructure both animate and inanimate. Water, for instance, the backbone of all peasant life, was an obvious target. Wells were poisoned, boreholes sabotaged, water engineers had their throats cut. In the remote villages of this 2,000 kilometre-long narrow country with its extremely poor north-south communications, these were, in the early years, often seen as isolated tragedies.

Zimbabwe, immediately after independence, began to suffer the same pattern of what at first appeared to be isolated incidents of banditry, with attacks, for example, on white commercial farms. The Zimbabwean economy, the oil pipeline from Mozambique, and lines of communication, were prime targets for sabotage, as were ZANU officials and symbols of the new government's authority, such as military posts. For instance a massive explosion in the Inkomo military barracks outside Harare destroyed $36 million of armaments in the summer of 1981. A few months later a bomb ripped through the ZANU party headquarters, killing six passers-by and injuring more than 100 people. A meeting of the country's leaders was due to take place in the building at that time, but had been postponed at the last minute. Sabotage from inside the largely unchanged security system of the new country was linked to South African military forces, some of whom were former Rhodesian soldiers who had left the country to serve within the SADF. Captain Frank Gericke, who was in charge of the armoury, was arrested after the Inkomo explosion, but mysteriously released during his questioning by a Detective Inspector named Frederick Varkevisser, with whom he managed to leave Zimbabwe in a light plane for South Africa.

Pretoria tacitly admitted involvement with the Inkomo explosion and Captain Gericke emerged later serving as an SADF officer.

The Matabeleland violence of this early period was almost invariably presented to the world as tribal fighting. An additional propaganda point stressed by the Western press was that the government troops involved were North Korean trained. Racist stereotypes of Korean brutality were strongly accentuated and the socialist character of the Pyongyang regime emphasized. The continuation of British military training teams was generally perceived as necessary because of the inadequacy of the North Korean training team. Meanwhile much of the brutality in the region by the dissidents took an almost identical form to the terror by mutilation, especially of women, used by MNR.

The South Africans had sent the MNR's Alfonso Dhlakama on a European tour in late 1980, showing the pattern of external support which would later emerge for MNR. In parallel, European links were being forged for UNITA; for the anti-SWAPO South African-backed Namibian leadership; for Joshua Nkomo, in a more ambiguous way, in his period of bitter denunciation of Mugabe; and for shadowy Zimbabwean dissident forces, said to be linked to the US-based Reverend Ndabaningi Sitole and operating out of Malawi. Dhlakama went to Portugal, West Germany and France and met representatives of conservative politicians such as Valéry Giscard d'Estaing and Franz Josef Strauss. This was the first cautious move by Pretoria and its allies towards an international attempt to legitimize the South African-generated opposition to the legal independent governments of Mozambique and Angola. The same network would later (in 1986–7) be used for the illegal South African puppet 'transitional government' of Namibia.

And in 1986 the US-based World Anti-Communist League organized a meeting at Jamba for all these groups and other US allies of the same political stamp, such as the Nicaraguan 'contras' and the Afghan mujahidin. There was no doubt about the US approval for illegal entry of these people into Angola – a telegram of support from President Reagan was read out to the meeting.

In late 1981 MNR documents were captured in the Garagua MNR military base in Manica province adjoining Zimbabwe, and according to them that year had seen the start of a determined ground offensive in Mozambique organized by South Africa. An estimated 10,000 fully armed and trained men had been either ferried in from South Africa or were part of the group hastily pushed over the border from the old Rhodesian bases, in the immediate aftermath of the Zimbabwe election. The South African liaison officers had, according to the Garagua documents,* a clear military approach to enfeebling independent Mozambique.

One part of the rationale for the cold-blooded destruction was only to appear later, when Pretoria demanded the expulsion of the African National Congress from Mozambique, claiming a security threat from ANC guerrillas infiltrating over the border into South Africa. The underlying policy goal of transformation of the independent state of Mozambique into a kind of Bantustan, like taxfree Ciskei, for instance, took even longer to emerge. It was first revealed publicly in 1984 in the Nkomati non-aggression pact that Mozambique signed with South Africa, expelling most of the ANC personnel in Maputo.

But, in 1981, FRELIMO suddenly faced its first serious challenge from an MNR which was installed by the South Africans in fortified bases in the south of the country. It was able under South African leadership to make hit and run attacks to sabotage road and rail links from Zimbabwe through central Mozambique to the sea, it was equipped to stage random terror attacks in urban areas such as Maputo and Beira, and, finally, it took to kidnapping foreigners as a propaganda tactic.

Between 1981 and 1987 well over 100 foreigners were subject to MNR attacks. Thirty-four were murdered and about seventy kidnapped. The people involved came from Britain, Brazil, Bulgaria, Cape Verde, China, France, both East and West Germany, Italy, Ireland, Portugal, Romania, the Soviet Union, Sri Lanka, Sweden, the US, Zimbabwe. Most of the

---

Destructive Engagement: Southern Africa at War, edited by Phyllis Johnson and David Martin, Zimbabwe Publishing House, 1986.

victims were civilian technicians and included a dozen nuns and priests. Most of them were released in Malawi to the International Red Cross after weeks or months of captivity.

In Angola UNITA has also used the kidnapping of foreigners as a means of publicity, starting in 1983 with sixty-four Czech nationals taken from the paper factory at Alto Katumbala. More successfully than MNR, UNITA used Westerners as bargaining chips for international recognition. Britain, for instance, in May 1984, sent Foreign Office Deputy Under Secretary Sir John Leahy to Savimbi's Jamba headquarters just north of the Caprivi Strip, to negotiate the release of sixteen British hostages; they had been taken prisoner a few months earlier in the Kafunfo diamond mines at the other end of the country on the Zaïre border. In a second raid on Kafunfo in December 1984 UNITA took twenty-two foreign hostages, including three British technicians. They were marched through the bush in Western Zambia for weeks before being released in March 1985.

Attacks on foreigners at the mines became epidemic in the mid-1980s and illustrated three strands of UNITA's tactics: publicity, economic sabotage of Angola's second most important export, and the secret use of neighbouring Zaïre, which paralleled, though predated, MNR's use of Malawi. Kidnapping itself was an extraordinarily successful propaganda trick and, curiously, brought UNITA little hostile comment on the terrible suffering and deaths of civilian women and children, in particular among the group of sixty-four Czech hostages taken in 1983 and held for over a year. (Nor was there public outrage over the murder of a Swedish aid worker kidnapped and killed in late 1987.)

Diamond production in Angola is just one simple indicator of the economic toll taken by the years of war and destabilization. The mines output had dropped by 1977 to only 15 per cent of what it had been in the last years of colonialism. It continued to sink still further while costs rose. UNITA pressure meant both the need for replacement of destroyed machines, and increasingly the need to supply the remote diamond towns by air, because of the threat of ambush of supply convoys on the long overland route from the coast. The laying of mines on roads and railways, like the destruction of machines, was just one aspect of infrastructural sabotage which touched equally dams, electricity pylons and factories all over Angola. In response to the crumbling official economy black markets flourished, like one just over the Zaïre border, where a thriving commercial centre was a clear sign of the success of a diamond smuggling racket. A long-running, intermittent trial of diamond smugglers in Luanda in the mid-1980s produced a cat's cradle of contradictory indictments, including some which ran into high reaches of the military and government, and others, less ambiguous, which linked to major Portuguese interests dating back to the colonial period.

Similarly, in Mozambique, the considerable financial interests of substantial business families, such as the Jardims and the Bulhoas, were unequivocally linked to Portugal and South Africa and to the funding and publicizing of MNR.

For financial empires like these the logic of continued South African dominance of the region was taken for granted. Other powerful economic barons based partly in South Africa, such as the giant Lonhro, hedged their bets on the shape of the future by cultivating high-level government connections; they also moved some management expertise into the devastated agricultural and tourism sectors in Mozambique in the mid-1980s, and made some overtures in Angola too. Burning of crops, mining of farmland, and physical attacks on women working in the fields in both Mozambique and Angola sent agricultural production plummeting, and were compounded by the drought and the plagues of locusts that ravaged the major part of the continent in 1983-4. Outside the region the catastrophic famine was too often blamed on mismanagement and early commitments to collective farming rather than on the crippling wars.

Meanwhile, SADCC attempted economic co-operation among the nine nations of the region who were trying to free themselves from the traditional transport infrastructure which reinforced South Africa's effort to build a constellation of states, but was never expected by most outsiders to have long-term success. Major donors privately thought that the SADCC's new or improved infrastructure would serve only as a temporary substitute for the traditional links, while South Africa itself changed and the wars against its neighbours abated.

The colonial period had left major infrastructural links between South Africa and both Mozambique and Angola which were even more critical to the country's industrial dominance than the railway routes. Ruacana hydro-electric station on the Angolan/Namibian border and Cahora Bassa in Mozambique were conceived as integral parts of South Africa's and occupied Namibia's power grid. Both suffered near closure from the wars. This obscured South Africa's real and long-term interests in them, while at the same time bringing their capital value so low that, in the event of fundamental changes in the respective governments they would be rewarding targets for South African private capital to take over completely.

Cahora Bassa is on the great Zambezi river in the highlands of Tete province in northwest Mozambique. It is the world's sixth largest hydro-electric project. It was planned ten years before Mozambique's independence and work continued throughout the liberation war and did not finish until Mozambique had been independent for two years. A decade later it was working at a mere one per cent of capacity with four of the five turbines out of action. The project was partly designed to provide 10 per cent of South Africa's own electricity needs on an 870-mile powerline to Johannesburg. But 500 of the 4,000 pylons were destroyed by MNR on this line alone. Power for industry and mechanized, irrigated agriculture for Mozambique envisaged an integration of the two economies. Mozambique was to take its power, not directly from Cahora Bassa, but off the South African state power grid, Escom. Similarly, Ruacana Dam in Namibia, and Lesotho's Highland Water Project, both big hydro-electric plants, were designed in the same logic of integration.

But in the aftermath of independence, even before the setting up of SADCC, Mozambique set to work as a priority to explore the economics of disengagement from South Africa. Migrant labour and transport were the two key areas; the power supply was to have been examined later. The assassination of the academic and journalist Ruth First, by a letter bomb sent to her office in the University in Maputo, served a number of ends for South Africa. She was a well-known member of the ANC and her work on Mozambique's economic alternatives were blazing a trail for the region. Her murder sowed fear and was a warning to others of the personal price payable for such concrete work against South Africa's interests. Across the continent in the southern Angolan town of Lubango another letter bomb killed Jeanette Schoon, also an ANC woman teaching in a university who had connections in Britain and elsewhere in Western Europe. This too, inevitably, magnified the fear of others who might have planned years of teaching in remote, underequipped, newly independent Southern African institutions that they too might be murdered by Pretoria's agents.

These two carefully targeted murders followed another, equally revealing of Pretoria's goals and capacity for infiltration. Joe Gqabi, the ANC's Zimbabwe representative, was assassinated outside his house in Harare in 1981. According to Prime Minister Mugabe, the murder, with Israeli Uzi submachine guns and a silenced pistol abandoned at the scene, was committed by former Rhodesian Selous Scouts sent in to Zimbabwe from South Africa. Zimbabwe's own security forces, and notably Geoffrey Price, an adviser to Mugabe himself who escaped to South Africa through Britain, supplied the intelligence for Gqabi's murder. Price's key role in South Africa's destabilization of newly independent Zimbabwe was later admitted by the South Africans. Two of his recruits, Colin Evans and Philip Hartlebury, were arrested by the Zimbabweans and charged with espionage. Both admitted supplying information about Gqabi and to having been recruited by Price to spy for South Africa. The South African government admitted their importance when, in January 1982, they made two offers to exchange the two men: first, for 115 Angolan prisoners; then for the Angolans plus one Soviet national. Both proposals were rejected by Zimbabwe.

The kind of destabilizing power that South Africa could exert inside Zimbabwe was deeply intertwined with the continuing

British influence in the security services, the civil service and even the judiciary. For instance, the cases against the two British citizens, Evans and Hartlebury, were, to the astonishment of the government, dismissed by a High Court judge, Mr Justice McNally. They were then detained under emergency powers. They were in the end freed, through Britain acting as an intermediary.

This case, like Matabeleland's troubles, had the dual effect of obliging the Mugabe government to be ruthless in moving against any dissent while, at the same time, fighting a rearguard action against a rising tide of hostility in the Western press against precisely this ruthlessness. Like every other Front-line State Zimbabwe's ability to fight a shadowy propaganda war against both South Africa and the Western press is poor.

None of the forms of destabilization would be so devastatingly effective without the ambitious and expert torrent of propaganda poured from South Africa into the world's major networks.

The propaganda machine is many-faceted. Over the post-independence period it has perfected for the world a generalized picture of incompetent black government all over Africa and particularly in the Front-line States. These governments are portrayed as beset by internal squabbles based on tribal differences, and as living proof of the failure of the economic options they have chosen. The broad outlines of this caricature are drawn in the embassies and aid missions of Western countries, where most Western reporters find ready confirmation of a simple picture, one that fits their own ideological preconceptions more readily than the complex and ugly realities of independent Southern Africa's struggle for survival on its own terms. An important facet of this picture is the contrast with successful, efficient, articulate white government in South Africa and the West. Even Western embassies themselves in Southern Africa, with their air-conditioning, swift international communications, private electricity generators, security staff and lavish casual entertainment, reinforce the contrasting stereotypes. It is an extraordinary testimony to the power of propaganda that for so long South Africa and its

Western backers could be generally seen, not as partners in the destruction of the infrastructure of half a continent, but as actors in a peace process.

These crude pictures are reflected back into Africa by the Western radio stations, which are part of the everyday diet of African decison-makers and of opinion-creators in national media. At a cruder level, powerful South African radio transmitters have been used to bombard local populations with lies. Radio Truth for the Zimbabwe dissidents, Voice of Free Africa for MNR, Voice of the Black Cockerel for UNITA, regularly retail stories of battles, government deaths and diplomatic support for the rebels, which are dreamed up in South Africa. At the same time these radio stations are used for wider ideological propaganda purposes. There is frequent favourable reference to South Africa, Israel and the United States and equally frequent condemnation of Soviet policies, the threat posed to Western interests by the presence of Cuban troops in Angola, and an alleged Soviet plan for dominance in the region. It is astonishing that for years the BBC's monitoring service has printed and distributed the transcripts of these broadcasts side by side with those of government radios in Luanda, Maputo and Harare as though the two versions had equal credibility.

Another contributor in the disinformation process is UNITA's Lisbon headquarters. Savimbi's spokesmen over the years grew more and more skilful at releasing communiqués close to deadlines, cultivating individuals in powerful news organizations, and using the policy of kidnapping foreigners as a way of publicizing its shadowy organization and forcing governments to negotiate with it for the release of their nationals. MNR, several years behind, had by the mid-1980s got the same Lisbon network working efficiently to broadcast its claims of towns taken and government forces killed or routed. They began even to send Western journalists on MNR trips into parts of Mozambique, a tactic perfected by Savimbi whose press conferences in Jamba, or even further inside Angola at Mavinga, invariably upstage official Angolan attempts to court the Western press.

The US hand in such misinformation has rarely been visible.

but there are plenty of examples that illustrate how seriously the process is taken and what devious routes are used for planting stories. The Church Committee in Congress inquiring into the relationship between the CIA and the media reported that in the mid-1970s the CIA owned outright more than 240 media operations and had many hundreds of foreign correspondents on its payroll. In the specific case of Angola just before independence, the former CIA agent John Stockwell detailed some of the lengths his team went to in manufacturing stories for planting in the press.* A whole department worked on a range of stories, from relatively small-scale incidents, such as supposed rapes carried out by Cuban troops in Angola, up to important falsifications of the historical record to be used in future policy-making. The pretence that Cuban combat forces arrived in Angola ahead of South Africa's invasion is one classic case of such a rewriting of history which, by being repeated often enough in the media, has effectively obscured the truth.

There was more in the same vein in early 1984, in the month before the watershed Nkomati pact was signed between Mozambique and South Africa: the *Sunday Times* in London ran a major article on the progress of the US brokered diplomatic moves in the region. Its thesis, briefly, was that the Soviet Union had suffered a major setback in Southern Africa because the Angolan government had turned to the United States as a peacemaker. The article cited a document supposedly captured by the Americans during their invasion of the island state of Grenada the previous October. It purported to be a record of a conversation between the then Angolan Foreign Minister Paulo Jorge and a Grenadian official; in it Paulo Jorge described his keen desire to relieve Angola of responsibility for SWAPO's guerrillas because they, according to him in this document, were responsible for the destruction of the Angolan economy. Paulo Jorge was at that period the Angolan official most frequently and openly cited by America as the main stumbling block to the peace pact they hoped the Angolans would sign with South Africa. The Foreign Minister,

In Search of Enemies, André Deutsch, 1978.

who was frequently at the United Nations in New York, was the best known Angolan voice protesting about the destruction of Angola's economy; but it was not due to SWAPO, as he was alleged to have said to the unnamed Grenadian, but to the South Africans who, he invariably commented, were supported and encouraged by the Reagan administration. The unearthing of such a dubiously sourced document so useful for US policy needs in the area at that precise moment should have caused the *Sunday Times* to question its authenticity. But it was printed without a caveat. No denial by the Angolan Minister would ever emerge in the Western press to set the record straight.

In the destabilization of Rawlings' Ghana too there were open attempts by US officials to use the local and international press to increase internal tensions and to delegitimize the government. One such move, in November 1982, was made the day before an attempted coup in which US involvement would later emerge; the US embassy in Accra and European news agencies used journalists in the Togolese capital of Lomé to publicize a damaging resignation letter from a top military official. The official, Brigadier Nunoo Mensah, then Chief of Defence Staff, left the country for Europe after the failure of the coup attempt and later became a leading figure in the web of disinformation linked to further US-backed coup plots further sapping the government's strength.

The Americans were sufficiently disturbed by the amount of information leaking out about their involvement in this series of linked plots to hold press conferences in London and elsewhere in Europe; in them State Department officials went to considerable lengths to persuade journalists that such information from Ghanaian officials was part of a Soviet disinformation campaign in Africa against the US.

The history of the US policy of constructive engagement in the whole region (examined in the next chapter, with particular reference to the Nkomati peace pact between Mozambique and South Africa) similarly has as its centrepiece the continuous and successful American manipulation of international public opinion.

One of the most carefully constructed parts of the regional

disinformation campaign concerns Namibia. Every element of weakness in the Front-line States which made them vulnerable to misinformation and confusion was particularly marked in the case of Namibia. There SWAPO had to cope with over-stretched cadres, poor communications from the Luanda headquarters, and a diplomatic battle in which the US deployed such weighty players as Mrs Jeanne Kirkpatrick, General Vernon Walters and Dr Chester Crocker.

Outside Central Hall, Westminster, one spring day in 1987, a group of pickets waited for participants in a UN conference on Namibia. The young students were handing out leaflets for the International Society for Human Rights, one of the most aggressive lobbying groups of the new right to have surfaced in Britain in the battle for influence in Southern Africa. With all the confidence of a new convert to a religious sect one snappily dressed youth pressed on SWAPO's Secretary for Foreign Affairs, Theo-Ben Gurirab, a leaflet accusing SWAPO of brutal torture, horrific conditions of incarceration, murders and disappearances. Gurirab, a large, soft-spoken man, stopped to ask them gently why they were so concerned about Namibia, whether they had ever been there, and whether they knew about the atrocities of the SADF in the country. With blithe unconcern the students outlined plans to visit Namibia and spoke of their concern for individual human rights every-where. On the same theoretical basis the conservative British student leader, Harry Phipps, had previously joined a group visiting the Nicaraguan 'contras'.

The background of the ISHR goes some way to explain the bigotry of its youthful adherents, the efficiency of its public relations and its well-funded publications. (These resorted to such tricks as use of the UN logo, SWAPO colours and a booklet similar in outward style to one published by Oxfam.) ISHR ruthlessly and skilfully pressed the legitimacy of the transitional government in Windhoek and, by 1987, it had even forced the issue of the expulsion of SWAPO representa-tives from the country on to the public agenda in Britain and West Germany.

The ISHR was founded in West Germany in 1981, an outgrowth of a Society for Human Rights started in Frankfurt a decade earlier. But its antecedents go back even further to an organization of Russian emigrés in the 1930s called the Narodno-Trudowo Sojus (NTS), originally formed to oppose the Russian Revolution of 1917 by engaging in acts of terror. ISHR's General Secretary, Ivan Agrusov, was an NTS member who served in the Nazi police force in the occupied areas of the USSR during the Second World War. NTS members inside the Soviet Union during the war worked hard on anti-Soviet propaganda. After the war Agrusov and five others, later to participate in the ISHR leadership, remained active in NTS. It was the the most prominent emigré organization to emerge during the cold war of the 1950s, and worked with tourists and businessmen visiting the Soviet Union. However Agrusov himself had to remain outside the country because he was wanted for alleged criminal activities during the occupation.

In the early 1980s ISHR began to publicize lack of free speech and movement in various socialist countries, such as the Soviet Union, Cuba, the German Democratic Republic, Vietnam, Afghanistan and Nicaragua. With the elaboration of the Reagan Doctrine during President Reagan's first years in the White House and the US's overt goal of reversing the gains of national liberation struggles all over the world, ISHR became a convenient vehicle for propaganda on many fronts. At its 1986 annual general meeting there were representatives of the Mozambique National Resistance as well as the anti-Sandinista Nicaraguans. But, because of the ISHR base in West Germany, with its historical links to Namibia, SWAPO was its prime target.

In parallel with the dominance within the Reagan administration of the views of its United Nations representative, Jeanne Kirkpatrick, the ISHR began to attack the legitimacy of SWAPO as the UN-recognized representative of the Namibian people. Accusations about SWAPO's human rights practices were rife in Britain as in West Germany. A 'Parents' Committee', set up in the Namibian capital Windhoek, began sending telegrams to many influential Western newspapers and public figures and even visiting West Germany and Britain under the auspices of ISHR. They were also working in close co-operation with the South African-funded and controlled public relations offices of the transitional government in Windhoek; this was trying to get UN resolution 435 dropped from the international agenda.

At the same time ISHR publications began to stress human rights violations in South Africa. But the emphasis was on illegal imprisonment, torture, and murder, not that perpetrated by the white regime, but by the 'comrades' linked to the United Democratic Front and the African National Congress. Photographs of horribly scarred and mutilated people purported to be victims of punishments meted out by the 'comrades' were widely circulated by ISHR. Published reports of an ISHR visit to South Africa claimed that the majority of South Africans were against sanctions and in favour of increased economic links between South Africa and Western capital. During its visit the ISHR delgation made much of its meetings with Chief Gatsha Buthelezi and the leaders of the nominally independent homelands. One member of the delegation, with disproportionate weight as the only African, was Pastor N.M. Musa. His previous career was as publicity secretary in Mr Ian Smith's Rhodesian campaign, in co-operation with the Selous Scouts, against the liberation movements ZANU and ZAPU.

In both West Germany and Britain Conservative MPs were by 1986–7 simultaneously preparing demands for increased government assistance to Namibia as though UN Resolution 435 were defunct, the country already an independent entity, and the war and South African occupation over. At the same time ISHR propaganda against SWAPO moved into higher gear; for instance it issued a press release claiming that SWAPO President Sam Nujoma had struck a Namibian woman, Mrs Talita Schmidt, across the face in the European Parliament building, when she tried to approach him to ask about children who were detained or had disappeared. A revealing chain of influence lies behind this seemingly trivial incident. Accompanying Mrs Schmidt on her tour, which had been organized by ISHR, was a former SWAPO member. Phil Ya Nangoloh, Secretary of Information and Publication for the SWAPO-Democrats party of Andreas Shipanga, was originally sent by SWAPO for education in Moscow. But he left his studies, was befriended by Lutheran church people in Finland,

and was next heard of living in a hotel in Park Avenue, New York. He then worked for one of the Reverend Sun Moon's right-wing publications in the US before returning to Namibia to work against SWAPO and for the South African-backed SWAPO-D. It was a propaganda feat that such a minor incident, but nevertheless involving SWAPO's leader, could make headlines in the Namibian press and get broadcasts throughout the world on the BBC although it never actually happened. Again, as in so many cases, no denial could undo the damage done to the organization's image.

The ISHR went on to pursue a highly successful campaign, particularly among European MPs, including British ones, of all parties, for the release of what they called the 'SWAPO one hundred' held in appalling detention conditions. Among the British MPs who promised support, particularly during the hectic days of a British election campaign in the summer of 1987, were even well-known SWAPO supporters. The skilful propaganda had sufficiently confused such people for them to assume that those detained were SWAPO members being held by the South Africans, rather than mostly fictitious people allegedly held by the liberation movement itself.

The American New Right, led by Heritage, encouraged by the Reagan administration, backed by a Conservative British government, and serviced by a wide range of subservient media, had put unprecedented effort into resetting the agenda on Southern Africa. But although the propaganda was largely successful outside the area, even harsher measures were to be employed to force conciliation across the region.

Chapter 8

The deception of Nkomati

On the morning of 20 October 1983 President Samora Machel, leader of the Marxist party FRELIMO, dressed conventionally for a State visit which included meetings with the Queen and the Prime Minister of Britain, made an early start at Claridges. In a private room adjoining his first floor suite he hosted a small breakfast party intended to give British newspaper editors the opportunity to hear his off-the-record assessment of the Southern Africa situation, and to break through the stereotyped image of Mozambique. Fleet Street had predictably and triumphantly hailed the President's London visit as proof that Mozambique was turning to the West to replace its long-standing Soviet connection. And even the small group of long-time FRELIMO supporters in Britain, who had gathered in the cold on the pavement outside Claridges to welcome the President, was somewhat pessimistic and confused. Had the enormous pressures – military, economic and social – which FRELIMO was not very successfully facing induced a sea change in the political attitudes of the leadership?

Few editors arrived in person for the 8 a.m. meeting in Mayfair, but sent junior representatives. Orange juice, toast or a traditional English breakfast appeared with the effortless efficiency of London's regular host to heads of state. Fernando Honwana, the President's gentle and earnest British-educated aide, with long experience of the British media, was at the small table, translating so effortlessly that the language barrier could be forgotten. President Machel, warm and smiling as usual at the start, turned rapidly waspish at the first two questions.

Predictably the first one was an invitation to denounce Marxism as an ideology and the Soviet Union for being ineffective as an ally of battered Mozambique. Still smiling, though visibly irritated, President Machel responded crisply that for Mozambique to send officers to Sandhurst or British-run training facilities in Zimbabwe implied no shift away from loyal friends and arms suppliers in Eastern Europe, those who had been constant both before and after Mozambique's independence. A friendly visit to Britain implied, he went on, no preference for Britain's multi-party democracy over FRELIMO's methods of ensuring grass roots democracy with elections in the villages, the districts and the provinces for a People's Assembly in accordance with a Marxist–Leninist organizational pattern.

The second question began to show the meeting going badly awry. Asked how serious was the threat to the country from South African-backed guerrillas of the Mozambique Resistance Movement, the President launched a sharp attack on the entire Western press for giving credibility to the 'armed bandits'; by implication at least, he virtually denied that there was a real military challenge to be fought off. Immediately the cordial atmosphere of the meeting deteriorated into the mistrust common between the Western press and African officials. Various journalists sought to reformulate the question. They were aware that it would be impossible to return to their offices with the news that, after all that had been written about sabotage and attacks in Mozambique, there was, according to the President, no real deterioration in the country's security situation, and therefore no crisis, no story.

But at that moment an aide came in and whispered to Honwana, and the subject of the conversation changed to the early morning news bulletin. This had led with the deepening crisis within the left-wing government on the Caribbean island of Grenada, where the Prime Minister, Maurice Bishop, had been freed from house arrest apparently by the spontaneous action of a huge crowd.

As speculation about the possibility of Bishop regaining power passed back and forth across the table Honwana began to look stricken. Then, in his soft voice and perfect English, he said that Maurice Bishop had been shot dead, according to the latest reports. The President was the first to respond, dropping his guard for a moment. The shock and pain were clear on his face and in his voice questioning how it was possible, what had happened. Of course no one present knew the answers and for most of the journalists it was just another story of the collapse of a controversial left-leaning regime in an obscure part of the world. But President Machel, like everyone who had known Maurice Bishop personally, responded with incredulity that this man's vivid personality and his extraordinarily bold political ideals, with their implications far beyond the Caribbean, could simply have been wiped out, and by his own close colleagues.

How much President Machel had valued Maurice Bishop's personal friendship and been strengthened by his courage had been clear, when only a few months earlier the Mozambican President had visited the tiny island of Grenada. Before the completion of the new Cuban-built airport, which was Bishop's pride and joy because it symbolized the release of the island from its status as a remote backwater, a journey to Grenada then was not a simple undertaking. The old airport, inconveniently sited on the far side of the island from the capital, St George's, could take only small planes: visitors had either to change planes, usually in Barbados, or take a long flight from Havana.

Chris Searle, a British teacher who had worked in schools and designed adult literacy programmes both in newly independent Mozambique in the mid-1970s and in Grenada after Bishop's New Jewel Movement seized power in 1979, wrote a moving account of the Grenadian response to President Machel's visit:

In early May we heard what for us was tremendous news. Samora Machel, the President of Mozambique, where we had worked for two years, was coming to Grenada to celebrate Africa Liberation Day at a rally in Seamoon Stadium near Grenville, on May 23rd. Seamoon is an old race track next to the blue and white of the crashing surf, winding in and out of tall coconut trees. It had been the venue of some of the huge anti-Gairy rallies of the early seventies and had a tradition of struggle. I had last seen

Samora Machel in Nampula, northern Mozambique, when he visited our school in July 1977. I had also heard him make a three hour speech at Nampula Stadium, delivered with a phenomenal physical energy, including dance steps, wide gesticulations, pacing the platform and snatches of songs.

On the day before the rally I had written this for the *Free West Indian*:

This weekend history is being made again in Grenada. Africa and the Caribbean will be united in love and solidarity. The rupture of history will be healed and the blood of a united people will flow again through a reconciliation that only revolution can bring.

I knew the Grenadian people would love Samora, and they did. He arrived, hand in hand with Maurice, and even though he spoke in Portuguese, soon had the enraptured attention of thousands of people. When he started to pace from one end of the long platform to the other, leaving the microphone standing alone in the centre, the listeners followed him with their collective eye, waiting for his next word which they couldn't understand in their heads, but understood completely in their hearts. One part of this speech I remember emphatically, and I was testing out my forgotten Portuguese. He said that the people must never for one second relax their vigilance, that the imperialist enemy was everywhere and comes in all colours and can strike at any time. As this was translated it lost some of its pungency, but it still struck home to those present. As he finished his speech and sang *Kannimambo*, the song we knew so well from Mozambique, I found myself lifting up and waving Kevin, our second son, right over the heads of everyone as if he were a flag. It was a synthesis for us, the meeting of Grenada and Africa, the marriage of revolutions and two proud, brave peoples as one. I had never written anything prophetic before, but I felt that I could make a claim with the final words of that article of the day before:

*Those of us who are fortunate enough to experience it
will never forget it, and we shall carry it in our souls to
drive us onwards for the rest of our days.*

But even in these moments of elation in Grenada, the
edge of violence still grazed us. As we came home
through St Andrew's squeezed tight in a minibus, I
looked out of the window along the main route, over the
mountainous Grand Etang, to St George's. The forces
that Samora had been talking about had been out and
working. On every one of the posters that lined the road,
on the photograph of Samora his eyes and mouth had
been mutilated, scratched out. The joy made way for
anger and some worry too, as well as a greater understanding of his words. The battles he and his people were
fighting every day in Southern Africa were here in the
Caribbean too.*

That morning in Claridge's, although President Machel's
iron discipline ensured the breakfast meeting continued with
superficial normality to talk of Southern Africa, the human
and political tragedy beneath the surface gave it another
dramatic dimension.

No one present that morning could have forecast then that
President Machel's visit that week would mark the beginning
of the last stage of his struggle for personal survival. The
political survival of FRELIMO, its holding of state power, was
also on the line. But on the anniversary of Maurice Bishop's
death four years later, President Machel himself was to die in
an aircrash for which the South African government was
widely held responsible, and it was impossible then not to
believe that his passionate reaction to his friend's death had
contained a kind of clairvoyant identification. Sudden death is
part of the everyday experience of revolutionary politics. In
the old saying, a shadow had passed over his grave and his face
had briefly reflected it. President Sankara, who was murdered
almost exactly one year after Machel's death, had similarly fore-
seen a common fate for himself, when he spoke of the other two.

*From *Grenada Morning* by Chris Searle, Karia Press, 1987.

The parallel conditions which had impelled President Machel to take the time to visit Grenada went deep. Chris Searle was far from unique in seeing the close identification between the two young leaders. They, and Sankara too, were trying to build, virtually from scratch, on an appalling colonial legacy of under-development – to create a proud independent society where education and social justice were to replace a degrading poverty and economic dependence on powerful neighbours. All were under perpetual military threat: either directly from the United States, as in the case of Grenada, or indirectly from the regime in Pretoria (US-supported in fact, though not always in word) in the case of Mozambique. Burkina's military threats came from French and US allies, such as Mali, Togo and Ivory Coast. All knew that the price of success with their own people's socialist development would be escalating pressure on them from the West. The three inspired similar electric popularity in any mass gathering, not just at home but in their region. They had symbolic importance in such gatherings as the Non-Aligned Movement, which went far beyond the actual weight of their small countries, and reflected admiration for their courage in confronting enemies whose powers far outstripped their own. All tried to break through the hostility or indifference of public opinion in the West led by government and media, by direct personal contact with ordinary people. Maurice Bishop's visit to the United States shortly before he died was a triumphant popular success. A visit to Harlem drew vast crowds, while a long meeting with the senior executives of the *New York Times* appeared to have changed the paper's previously hostile atti-tude to the new government in Grenada. But, inevitably, or so he thought afterwards, this very breakthrough of consciousness at some levels of US society reinforced the antipathy of the US administration to him personally, and to the social experiment of the People's Revolutionary Government he headed.

During his October meetings in England with Mrs Thatcher, the Queen, defence personnel at Sandhurst and others, President Machel seemed increasingly confident that they had provided an even more significant kind of breakthrough. In Britain, as in the other six European countries he visited on that autumn trip, the President, his wife Graca, the Minister of

Education, Foreign Minister (later to be President) Joachim Chissano, and other officials, all repeatedly stressed that if the West would only commit diplomatic and financial aid to Mozambique instead of to South Africa, the government in Pretoria would reassess its policy of destruction of its neighbour and adopt a live and let live policy. It was the reasoning of logic, morality, desperation, not of *realpolitik*.

Britain, France, Portugal and the United States all played a part in persuading President Machel that the jigsaw of new relationships across Southern Africa envisaged by constructive engagement was a real possibility. Despite the deep divisions of opinion across Africa about whether the West would, or could, deliver even the first South African part of the bargain – independence for Namibia under UN Resolution 435 – Mozambique, in a specially vulnerable position, made the first move. President Machel became the first Front-line State leader to negotiate a deal with South Africa. Pretoria's policy of destabilization had achieved its ultimate goal – pacification.

At the border town of Komatipoort on 16 March 1984 President Machel met President P. W. Botha and ceremoniously signed a mutual non-aggression pact, to be known as the Nkomati agreement. It was to include the setting up of a Joint Security Commission composed of Mozambican and South African officers working together to monitor any infringements of the pact. Shockwaves went through the continent at what was widely perceived as a stunning reversal of history in the region. In an important symbolic gesture all the heads of state of the other Front-line States refused to attend the ceremony, notwithstanding a personal appeal to back it from President Machel. Within Mozambique too there were many mourners of this defeat presented as a triumph. In the sister republic of Angola there was acute concern that the agreement would be a precedent used by the West to put pressure on the rest of the region to capitulate to Pretoria. Angola, already partially under South African occupation, felt particularly vulnerable. But the worst blow was to the President of the African National Congress, Oliver Tambo, who had only been told by his old friend President Machel in a long and painful meeting in Maputo immediately before, that the majority of the African National Congress cadres based in the Mozambique capital would have to leave under the agreement. In less than three years the South Africans would force them all to leave. Tambo said publicly that the Mozambique leadership had been forced to choose 'between life and death. So if it meant hugging the hyena they had to do it.' The ANC leader knew that FRELIMO's survival was at stake.

Although Mozambique pledged to maintain exactly the same level of diplomatic support for the ANC, the extraordinary sight of FRELIMO soldiers entering the flats and offices of ANC personnel, taking away weapons and escorting ANC cadres to the airport, left scars of bitterness which did not heal overnight. Behind the gold-braided uniforms, the guards of honour, the celebratory champagne at Nkomati, President Machel's legendary smiles were uneasy for once and there was no rejoicing on the Mozambican side. Only in Pretoria, and in Washington where Dr Chester Crocker claimed President Machel as the best friend of the United States, was there the euphoria and excitement which accompanies the achievement of a long-worked-for difficult goal.

In fact, even as President Botha sipped his champagne at the meeting with President Machel on the border, his own military men knew it was only one side of South Africa's policy. In the weeks immediately before the agreement Pretoria had covertly infiltrated over the border into Mozambique hundreds of newly trained, well-equipped guerrillas from the Phalaborwa training camp. Some were veterans of the camps in Rhodesia dismantled in 1979. Many were former migrant workers from Mozambique scratching a living from South Africa's mining sector. South Africa had no intention of abandoning MNR. An undercover South African military team was sent into Zambezia province to train 100 MNR instructors and 200 recruits. A new transmission network was set up between SADF and the MNR. A resupply operation by the South African military using planes and ships was organized, intended to give the MNR autonomy for six months. While all this was being set up by the South African military it is not clear how far the South African politicians, in their various meetings with Mozambican leaders during the preparations for Nkomati, ever intended, even at this point, to diminish their support to MNR. Nor is it clear how the different strands of policy-makers in Washington saw the future options of FRELIMO, of MNR, and of Mozambique, as a result of the new regional situation created by Nkomati. One Western assumption was that the pact had broken the unity of the Front-line States in the confrontation with South Africa and put the ANC in a weakened diplomatic position.

The ousting of most of the ANC from Maputo under the terms of Nkomati was of symbolic importance to the South Africans, rather than actually changing the balance of forces in the region. Mozambique had never had ANC military bases or training camps in the country. The enforced expulsion was of course intended as a warning to those Front-line States which did, notably Angola and Tanzania.

Of more potential significance was the proposal, vigorously advanced by the US side, that South African and Western capital would be injected into Mozambique as a result of the non-aggression pact. To the ANC, and others in the Front-line States, this was an open attempt by South Africa to transform Mozambique, as an ANC communiqué put it, 'to the level of the Bantustan creations'.

To the more thoughtful proponents of constructive engagement in Washington, South African and Western capital could be the long-term answer to changing the character of the country, from Marxist–Leninist self-definition to a state closer in character to Swaziland, Malawi or Mauritius; in these states Western and South African capital was accepted on its own terms, that is, with the right to make high profits and export them home. The high level of exploitation of workers, the accompanying pay-offs, kickbacks and corruption of top officials, and the pliability of the state that is part of this Western economic package was so alien to the nationalist character of the Mozambique leadership that this aspect of Nkomati was, from FRELIMO's point of view, absurd. For a few weeks in Mozambique there was a flurry of visiting businessmen from South Africa, and a few from the West, and speculation that sections of the economy such as tourism and agriculture were to be transformed overnight. One of the most noted ambassadors for capitalism was Mr Tiny Rowland, chairman of the British Lonhro company, which had major interests in all the states bordering Mozambique (including South Africa). Lonhro promised the Mozambicans to revamp the beautiful old Polana hotel in Maputo overlooking the Indian Ocean and to invest in the all-important agricultural sector. The Mozambican authorities envisaged a British management team and an injection of capital which would have added casinos and other such magnets for international tourism. What they saw arrive on the Lonhro team was Portuguese, or former Portuguese (now South African) management. And in agriculture, where Lonhro's involvement (again using South African or Rhodesian management) did produce excellent results for the first year at Chokwe, President Machel's birthplace, results elsewhere were not dramatically successful. Overall the initiatives to attract new capital never flowered. Within a year Marxist Mozambique was looking to the IMF for help, and accepting conditions such as cutting the size of the army, raising prices and sacking civil servants.

The real constraint on private capital was the persistently precarious security. The publication of the Gorongoza documents, captured by a joint Zimbabwean/Mozambican force in August 1985 at the central MNR camp, revealed the background to this volatile security situation. The documents, which even South Africa did not try to claim were fabricated, revealed just how duplicitous the South Africans had been in their approach to the Nkomati agreement. To the embarrassment, though hardly the surprise, of the Reagan administration, Gorongoza, with all its ample documentation, fell to FRELIMO just before a visit to the United States by President Machel.

Several dozen kilos of documents were left behind by the MNR who fled when government troops attacked. Some were partially burned and were subsequently pieced together. A desk diary and two notebooks relating to the period from December 1983 to July 1985 revealed in detail the South African control of MNR, the attempt to promote the transition of the MNR from an extension of the SADF to a status of apparent independence. The documents showed the careful selection of economic sabotage targets, of foreign *co-operantes*, and of FRELIMO officials working in fields such as health, education and agricultural development as assassination targets. They revealed too the covert links whereby the MNR leadership was not only visited inside Mozambique by South African military and civilian officials at very high levels, but given aid to leave Mozambique via South Africa for diplomatic forays to various African and Western countries.

In the weeks immediately before Nkomati the diary has such incriminating entries as:

January 16: owing to the undertaking that the South Africans will make to Machel in the light of the talks underway, resupply for the first six months of '84 will come in the first three months . . . January 18: on behalf of the Commander in Chief to accompany the group of South African instructors; establish liaison between the instructors and our commanders . . . January 21: went to Malawi to talk to President Banda about the Russians (technical experts captured by MNR) and to take them to RSA . . . February 2: our friends must always speak English and not Afrikaans, to avoid soldiers finding out, as we have many fighters who were formerly workers in RSA . . . February 7: H. E. left for Pretoria at 1500 hours with the Secretary General for talks with the South African Generals, at their invitation . . . February 22: meeting in Pretoria between H. E. and the General of Military Intelligence; General of the Special Forces; Brigadier of Military Intelligence and Colonel Vaniker of Military Intelligence. Objective: planning the war in the face of the situation taken up by the South African Republic . . . February 24: the General will ensure resupply even after the agreement by SA with the communist Machel, especially ammunition and radio transmitters.

The diary goes on to pinpoint the economic (and infrastructure) targets for MNR attacks, including the Cahora Bassa hydro-electric complex, railways and SADCC projects. In the year and a half between the entries in the diary and its capture at Gorongoza every item in the target list was hit over and over again. Mozambique's estimated physical damage and loss of production over this period (1980–5) is US$5.5 billion. The officially estimated total for the nine-country SADCC region is $25–30 billion over the first six years of this decade. Put differently, destabilization and direct aggression costs total $400 for every child, woman and man in the whole region of Southern Africa. A quarter of a million of Mozambique's citizens were homeless refugees scattered over five borders.*

One evening in mid-1986 in the peaceful surroundings of the FRELIMO Party's hotel, the Rovuma, in Mozambique's extraordinarily quiet capital Maputo, the then Minister of Information Luis Jose Cabaco looked back at Nkomati. He had had the unenviable task of explaining it all over the world at the time, and had had to insist to deeply sceptical journalists working on the area as well as to officials in many countries that FRELIMO believed in South Africa's apparent change of heart and commitment to peaceful coexistence. Internally, however, he insisted there had been no illusions about what such a pact could effect. There had never been a real expectation that South Africa's imperative to crush its neighbours could be checked by a 'gentleman's agreement'. The detailed revelations of the deceptions the previous year in the Gorongoza documents had, he said, been shocking in their audacity, but not surprising. The Nkomati agreement had, to him, achieved two important goals. Firstly, it had headed off a South African attack on Maputo itself. FRELIMO intelligence had believed this was an imminent possibility at the time which could have meant the end of the FRELIMO government. Secondly, the outside world could, for the first time, see clearly that the roots of the continuing violence in the region lay in Pretoria. Again and again as evidence of South Africa's violations of the non-aggression pact were made public FRELIMO officials

*UNICEF report and SADCC documents by Professor Reginald Green, Institute of Development Studies, Sussex University.

refused to declare Nkomati as dead, and in fact reiterated their commitment to good neighbourliness with the existing regime in South Africa. Cabaco referred back to President Machel's visit to Britain in late 1984 when it had been clear how little knowledge or interest there was in Britain, as elsewhere in Europe, in the trials of being a neighbour to white South Africa. Later visits by President Machel to Japan and the United States had helped shift the diplomatic tide against Pretoria partly because of its growing external aggression, as well as because of its better-known internal repression. Gradually over 1986 and 1987, as the military situation inside Mozambique deteriorated, international support for FRELIMO grew in the West, though only by fits and starts.

Powerful opposition currents were also generated abroad. In late 1986 Gordon Jones, vice president for government and academic relations at the Heritage Foundation, predicted 'a real push in the conservative community in Washington to move aid for RENAMO (MNR) as we did for UNITA'. The Heritage Foundation is generally credited with being the fount of academic orthodoxy underlying the Reagan doctrine of rolling back communism all over the world. Other less well-known sources of funding and influence in Washington, such as the Conservative Action Foundation, also began open support for MNR just at the point when South Africa's role in destabilizing its neighbours was coming under sharp criticism internationally. Dr Bonner Cohen, research director of the Conservative Action Foundation, gave a pointer to the confidence and long-term aims of the MNR's backers when he said in early 1987, 'RENAMO is now about where UNITA was in 1984, but within the next couple of years we are confident that Congress will extend support to RENAMO as well.' Cohen was one of the backers of Jonas Savimbi's extensive and successful public relations work in the United States between 1985 and 1987.

MNR opened a lobbying office in Washington in mid-1986, working out of a suite in the Heritage Foundation building. MNR's extreme difficulty in finding credible leaders who were not actually Portuguese, in order to present its case to the international community, led to the office being run by an American, Thomas Schaaf. Schaaf was effective in influence building in Congress from the start. By mid-1987 twenty-eight senators, including a presidential candidate, Bob Dole, Republican Leader in the Senate, were backing MNR. In both the Senate and the House of Representatives conservatives advanced legislation which would put stringent preconditions on economic aid to Mozambique and other of the Front-line States. The proposals of one of the most extreme supporters of MNR, Representative Dan Burton, a Republican from the mid-western state of Indiana, give a flavour of the political atmosphere. Congressman Burton demanded that formal military facility agreements with the US (such as Kenya or Morocco have) and a top rating of voting with Washington in the UN should be the conditions for aid to African countries. He further demanded that emergency humanitarian assistance be administered by MNR as well as the government, and that aid agencies be encouraged to work with MNR. Fanciful claims that Cuban and even Ethiopian troops were fighting in Mozambique began to appear, unsourced, in papers such as the far-right's *Washington Times* (a paper linked to the Moonies). They fed suspicion of FRELIMO and put pressure on Mozambique from its supporters within Western institutions to deny its socialist basis.

In his attempt to create legitimacy internationally for MNR, Schaaf said himself that he concentrated on trying to give MNR some say in the distribution of incoming aid. This, of course, was a grotesque irony given that MNR itself, by its destruction of the infrastructure etc., had virtually created the very need for aid.

Schaaf was a prime mover in persuading aid agencies to meet MNR and to try and work with both sides, as though Mozambique's was a civil war. He even claimed in early 1987 that, 'the agriculture in the RENAMO-liberated zones is very productive. All recent media visits to RENAMO-held Mozambique have verified there is no starvation problem. The problem is in the communist areas of the country where people have been forcibly displaced. It is very similar to the Ethiopia situation where the Marxist–Leninist policies have caused a collapse of the economy.' The use of aid agencies as a political tool in the Southern African war was not new. For instance, in Savimbi's headquarters at Jamba on the Namibian border the French *Médecins Sans Frontiers* has long had medical teams – a clear political choice of ally by this aid organization. MSF was not therefore authorized by the MPLA to work in other needy areas of Angola. MSF was a contributing influence to the current of opinion in France which, faster than in the US and not merely on the far right, had by 1986 given Savimbi a new legitimacy as an authentic nationalist. It is no coincidence that MSF was the leading aid agency to denounce the policies of the Ethiopian government and to work against giving aid to that country.

In Mozambique MSF was one of several aid organizations wanting to work with all parties as the military and social crisis developed in 1986 and 1987. Most of them chose to act as though the war were civil war, not South African aggression using a proxy. Numerous international aid organizations were drawn to the refugee settlements in Malawi, Zambia and Zimbabwe and there were incidents of MNR recruitment in these camps. Access to MNR for aid workers was particularly easy in Malawi. But the most significant sign of change in the climate among the aid community came with a UNICEF report on the children in the Front-line States written in late 1986.

The UNICEF report, based on statistics researched by Professor Reginald Green of the Institute of Development Studies in Brighton and a long-time analyst of economic trends in the Front-line States, painted a devastating picture of societies not just in crisis but, judged by every social indicator, in chronic decline. For instance, in Angola and Mozambique the mortality rate for under fives had been reduced to 260–70 per 1,000 by 1980, five years after independence. (At independence 70 per cent of the population in both countries lived out of reach of any form of health care and therefore any possibility of statistical assessment.) Six years later, however, under-five mortality had risen to an estimated 325–75 per 1,000. Vaccination campaigns which were successful in the 1970s had slid back substantially a decade later. More than 40 per cent of health posts and centres were destroyed in the early 1980s. In education the story was the same. In Mozambique after independence there was a surge forward in adult literacy and primary school enrolment but, ten years later, at least 40 per cent of schools were destroyed and rural life so completely disrupted by the war that adult literacy classes had almost stopped.

UNICEF's conclusion in 1987 was that the children of Southern Africa need, above all, peace before there can be any hope of reinstating social services or development. Introducing this shocking report in London, James Grant, UNICEF's Director General, spoke of UNICEF's role in another war zone – El Salvador. He reminded his listeners that there UNICEF had organized a series of three-day 'vaccination truces' between the government of Napoleon Duarte and the guerrillas of the Democratic Revolutionary Front/Farabundo Marti Liberation Front. UNICEF had not yet, he said, approached the government of South Africa or the MNR with its report, but he and other UN officials left open the possibility of such an approach. Never before had such a senior and respected international body come so close, apparently, to advocating truce or peace talks.

In fact in May 1984, just two months after Nkomati, the first of two unofficial meetings took place between FRELIMO top officials and MNR leaders, one in Frankfurt and one in Pretoria, in which the government offered the MNR an amnesty. However, FRELIMO ruled out the MNR demand for a government of national reconciliation that would give them Cabinet posts and pave the way to a multiparty system. This outline of a political settlement was virtually identical to the US proposals for Savimbi to join the MPLA government in Angola, or for SWAPO to accept links with the various South African-backed elements in Namibia. The idea of compromise increasingly struck a sympathetic chord with many Western aid workers horrified by the terrible toll the regional war was taking. The psychological pressure mounted from Western sources on every private and public occasion, and at the same time the gulf of incomprehension widened; this was despite a surface improvement in relations between Britain's Conservative government and embattled Mozambique, which had begun with President Machel's visit to London in October 1983.

As Nkomati failed to bring economic, political or military respite from Pretoria, Mozambique remarkably managed to maintain good relations with one of South Africa's key allies, Britain. So good, in fact, were relations that in mid-1986 when the British Foreign Secretary Geoffrey Howe made an unsuccessful peace-seeking visit to the region it was Mozambique that allowed him at least to save face, with a warm political welcome. His ill-advised trip had been part of the British Government's attempts to stave off mandatory sanctions on South Africa. He had been humiliated by the ANC's refusal to meet him in Lusaka, during his regional tour.

In mid-1987 Joachim Chissano made his first visit to Europe as President of Mozambique. He spoke to a packed hall full of the British diplomatic, military and business establishment in the dowdy colonial-style surroundings of the Royal Institute for International Affairs, at Chatham House in London's St James's Square. Asked by one of the Sandhurst officers in the audience whether there was a possibility of meetings and reconciliation with MNR, President Chissano, as quiet and low key in public as President Machel had been ebullient, responded with an analogy. Suppose Mozambique, he said, came to Britain, recruited and took home for military training a handful of discontented people who were then brought back into Britain to perpetrate economic sabotage and terrorism against innocent civilians. Suppose, he went on, Mozambique then told the British government they should talk to these people. 'Would you talk? I wouldn't.'

Perhaps as he spoke he was thinking of the faces he had seen just before his visit to Britain during a trip to Zambezia, then the most desperately dislocated province in the country. Zimbabwean and Tanzanian troops fighting alongside Mozambicans had turned the tide in the southern part of the province and an estimated 40,000 people, hungry, ragged and disoriented, had been freed from MNR control. But they were freed into an economically devastated province, estimated to have only one quarter of its cattle left after massive slaughtering by MNR, and where the harvest in grain and oil seeds was down by at least half.

After flying in to a shattered little town called Nicoadala, President Chissano had stood in front of a huge crowd, accompanied by his Foreign Minister, formerly the Minister of Health, whose work in the early years of independence had made Mozambique, for many aid officials, the very model of what is possible. Now the hospital at Mopeia and the electricity station next to it – both burned to the ground – were just two examples of how those possibilities in Zambezia had been destroyed.

The President invited on to the rostrum nine women and children from those who had been kidnapped by MNR. They had survived the ripping apart of their families and the months or years of nomadic existence, moving on under the terror of rapes and beatings from the MNR bands. After they had spoken he summed up the common experience:

> We have seen that the bandits have wrecked the lives of people who could never do them any harm. They kidnapped children and abandoned them in the bush . . . houses are burned down and no one can understand why they burned them down . . . what country do they want to govern? One without people, without houses, without roads and infrastructures? [In South Africa too] the Boers do not hesitate to kill defenceless people.

Throughout 1986, as the level of violence rose inside South Africa, so the violations of Nkomati had become more flagrant and more ambitious. The success of Zimbabwean troops on holding open the railway line from Zimbabwe to the sea at Beira was beginning to change the freight dependency on South Africa. Partially in response to this success Malawian territory was used as a supply and logistics base for MNR incursions into Mozambique's Zambezia and Tete provinces, and had, by the middle of the year, gravely increased the threat to FRELIMO's survival. It was the same threat in a different guise as that from the direct South African invasion of the capital Maputo which had preceded Nkomati. Many times during 1986 in the wild remote province of Zambezia bands of several hundred MNR men had swept through the area, not just destroying infrastructure and killing, but even holding small towns. When FRELIMO counter-attacked the MNR again and again sought refuge over the border in Malawi. Several unsuccessful high-level delegations were sent by President Machel and Prime Minister Mugabe to the Malawian capital Lilongwe, to persuade the ageing and eccentric Dr Hastings Banda to cut aid and facilities for MNR. The Mozambican population, who mostly fled the bandits, was arriving in thousands on the coast. The province capital of Quelimane was swollen to many times its normal size while its supplies of every necessity were cut off, except by sea.

South Africa in fact made a push in 1986 to capture Quelimane. This would have given a new level of international legitimacy to MNR which would then be said to be holding a liberated area. It would have solved South Africa's economic and logistical problems of resupply through Malawi. For those such as the Heritage Foundation and Thomas Schaaf lobbying with aid officials and diplomats on behalf of MNR would have become suddenly much easier. Thousands of MNR soldiers, led by South Africans with blackened faces, invaded Mozambique in October 1986 in a quantitatively and qualitatively different kind of attack. This was not destabilization; it was a bid for power which raised the stakes in Mozambique and brought about another regional watershed as significant as Nkomati.

In early October, at a regional summit in Maputo, President Machel told the other Front-line presidents about the new South African threat from Malawi in emotional and dramatic terms. For the first time the Front-line States were faced with the real possibility not just of increased strain and weakness in one of their number, but the actual collapse of the state of Mozambique. As a result, one of FRELIMO's oldest friends, Tanzania, made a new level of commitment to Mozambique. The still fairly new President, Hassan Ali Mwinyi, the Party, and top military commanders decided that, in spite of Tanzania's extremely difficult economic situation, they would put troops into Mozambique. The Defence Minister, Salim Ahmed Salim, went on a tour of Africa, Scandinavia, Eastern and Western Europe to raise an international material support package which would allow Tanzania to move in troops.

When, within two weeks, President Machel, with other top Mozambican officials, flew to northern Zambia on the final trip of his life, this further regional summit clearly told Malawi to halt the support to MNR or face an economic blockade: paralysis of every route out of the landlocked country.

Flying home from the summit in Zambia President Machel's plane became locked on a false radio beacon in circumstances which were never clarified. The plane missed the signals from Maputo airport and crashed just inside South African territory. From the moment it hit the ground Pretoria began a massive campaign of disinformation and confusion. On the site of the crash, in the most heavily militarized area of South Africa, a large temporary campsite was swiftly removed and never explained. For four and a half hours, inexplicably, no one came to the crash site, although South African military radar had certainly tracked every movement of the presidential plane. Even then the first South African officials to arrive were not from the nearby military bases, but police, including at least one who spoke Portuguese. All night South Africa made no move to inform Maputo. At nearly 7 a.m. the following morning, when they did inform them, Pretoria said that the plane had crashed in Natal, not Transvaal. This resulted in even more time being lost before Mozambican officials got to the site, arriving well after South Africa's Foreign Minister, Pik Botha, who was accompanied by journalists. In the meantime the wreck and its surroundings had been ransacked by South African police and many documents taken away, although Mr Botha publicly informed the Mozambican Security Minister, Sergio Viera, at the crash site that nothing had been touched. Three weeks later Mr Botha produced on television documents which he claimed had been found in the plane's debris, which purported to be evidence of a plot by Zimbabwe and Mozambique to overthrow the government of Malawi. Mr Botha gave six press conferences in this period, effectively pre-empting the international inquiry into the crash by a tripartite commission composed of the Soviet Union, as the makers of the plane, Mozambique, as its owners, and South Africa, as the country in which the plane crashed. Besides the allegation of the plot against Malawi, he and other South African officials made a number of wild assertions, later completely disproved. The Soviet pilot, they said, was drunk, the plane had defective and old-fashioned equipment, the air traffic controllers at Maputo airport had been arrested and so on. All this obscured the fact that South Africa refused for weeks to release the black box flight recorder. A rival international inquiry, set up inside South Africa and including a former US astronaut and one Briton, unsurprisingly concluded that the crash had been an accident.

Unusually, the summit in Zambia, so crucial to the question of Malawi's future regional role in the South, had been announced a full week ahead. The South African military were put on full alert for forty-eight hours the day before it, and before the crash. The airports of Nelspruit and Komatipoort were strengthened with a squadron of Impala fighter-bombers and three each of Puma and Alouette helicopters. Reconnaissance commandos, new infantry units and armoured cars were moved into Komatipoort during the previous week.

As the shock of President Machel's death hit the Front-line States, President Kaunda of Zambia spoke for the region when he said that South Africa would be held 'guilty until proven innocent' of causing the crash. And Prime Minister Mugabe, in a moving speech to Parliament, committed Zimbabwe to fight alongside Mozambique to the last soldier. Reminding Zimbabweans of Mozambique's support during their own liberation war against the illegal government of Ian Smith, Mr Mugabe said, 'How many countries are so large-hearted? How many leaders have that vision? How many have that powerful commitment to take the sufferings of others as their own suffering?'

And Tanzania was quietly preparing for a new era of sacrifice. Party meetings all over the country discussed the country's military commitment to Mozambique. In remote and impoverished peasant communities, particularly southern Tanzania, spontaneous gifts of cloth, a chicken, part of the harvest, or a little money were offered for what no one believed would be a short war against South Africa. The era of

Nkomati's false promise of peace had definitely ended. Beside Mozambique in the war with South Africa, Zimbabwe and Tanzania had chosen to fight too rather than accept the defeat of a decade's hopes.

Chapter 9

Carrots and sticks

By 1987 confrontation within South Africa had risen to explosion point. The intricate web of organized extra-parliamentary opposition, which had begun with the campaign to boycott the tri-cameral parliament elections in late 1983 had flowered in the succeeding years. The successive states of emergency starting in June 1986, the arrests of some 30,000 people (including more than 18,000 children, some as young as eleven), the emergency detention of 11,000 children (more than half of whom testified to having been tortured by police), ruthless re-detentions (including those of twelve-year-old girls) as one emergency ended and another began, and street confrontations with security forces which left more than 2,500 people dead – all this amounted to civil war. In one period of early 1986 five people were being killed by police and troops on the streets every day.

The United Democratic Front (UDF), formed in August 1983, initially grouped about 600 organizations, ranging from church groups and community organizations to various regional organizations and ran joint campaigns with the trade union federation, COSATU. By 1987 UDF had an estimated two million members. The Front's basic policy document was a carefully-worded restatement of the 1955 Freedom Charter of the banned African National Congress, calling for a unitary democratic state based on the principle of majority rule. Only in 1987, when the UDF's solid support even among far from radical groups was judged to be unshakeable, did its leaders formally adopt the ANC's Freedom Charter itself.

Waves of arrests of the national and local UDF leaders, launched under each new phase of emergency rule, sent many of them underground to escape the detentions for which they

Zaire and neighbouring countries

were prime targets. UDF's organizational capacity was greatly hampered, but even some of the leaders themselves were surprised at the way the crisis itself proved a political forcing house for a wide spectrum of people, and produced layer under layer of leaders in many organizations. Each time local leaders were arrested or went underground new people emerged, ready to take over the leadership of the community, factory, school or union. The government later banned UDF itself, and most of its affiliated organizations, from receiving funds from abroad, in an effort to check mushrooming international support for this extra-parliamentary opposition. Continuous legal challenges to the arrests, to the torture, especially of child detainees, to the ban on receiving external funds, to the censorship which was imposed as much to lull its own white constituency as to lessen external pressure on the government, gave one indication of this new opposition's broad capacity to challenge the state on its own terms. Some of these challenges were successful in finding loopholes in the emergency laws. And for every closure of a loophole fresh legal challenges were raised by a growing section of the legal community.

At the same time, in spite of the military occupation of the townships, the white regime was unable physically to cripple the UDF. Its local affiliates increasingly organized mass actions such as rent strikes, bus strikes, stay-aways, school strikes and community education. The UDF mushroomed into the framework of an alternative state in this turbulent period before the government moved to crush it in early 1988. The African National Congress's leadership called in 1986 for the townships to be made 'ungovernable'. As more and more black collaborators with the administration were hounded from their homes and prevented from carrying out even such duties as rent collection it was clear that the ANC's Radio Freedom, beamed into the townships from Addis Ababa, Lusaka, Luanda and Maputo, was posing a challenge to authority which Pretoria could not meet. Underground military and political units of the ANC infiltrated into the townships and provided significant morale-building proof that the alternative organizations could successfully withstand the government's use of unprecedented levels of force against them. It was a measure of how far out of touch the government was that they were so surprised by the security forces' failure to deter people, despite the heavy personal price being paid by so many, from creating new organizations openly opposed to the government.

In early 1987, for instance, clandestine organization throughout the whole country was able, without one arrest, to bring three delegates from each region by plane, bus and train to a one-day conference in a university hall in Cape Town, where they formed a national Youth Congress, affiliated to the UDF. The South African Youth Congress (SAYCO) was a legal but completely underground mass movement with 600,000 members. It was an extraordinary phenomenon to have been produced out of such a background of deprivation and violence. It could be seen as a kind of urban parallel to the Ugandan youth movement during the five years of the second Obote period – young people who similarly abandoned the older generation's fatalistic acceptance of dictatorship and took up arms for an unprecedented civil war. There was a similarity also to the students of Burkina who made Sankara's grave a place of pilgrimage and refuted the new regime's rationalization for their coup. These street youths of South Africa were often unemployed and ill-educated but extraordinarily confident of their role as leaders and their responsibility within the townships. Giving delegates two days to get back to their home bases, the elected SAYCO leaders then gave a press conference announcing the formation of their organization. The leaders were photographed, named and quoted, but were then able to fade into the underground and even travel abroad and return successfully.

Two months later the UDF itself held its third, and secret, National Congress in Durban, successfully bringing together 200 delegates from nine regions throughout the country. Men like the UDF publicity secretary Murphy Morobe, who had defied the government by working underground for more than a year, were able to attend. (Morobe was caught and detained shortly afterwards.) It was at this 1987 UDF congress that a psychological Rubicon was crossed: it was decided to examine openly the possibility of the UDF endorsing the ANC Freedom Charter as the blueprint for a post-apartheid society. The cautious lawyer's wording of this decision – which had been under discussion since UDF's inception – was a hallmark of the UDF leadership's tactic of moving slowly enough in its confrontation with the government to bring into the opposition a middle ground of the society. The ANC leaders abroad were, in the same period, similarly careful to cultivate a moderate image and gain a range of influential non-revolutionary allies. The fracturing of the white opposition to President Botha, with many of them moving closer to the ANC, was one measure of this success at home. Abroad too the ANC gained ground even in conservative political and business circles.

The Durban UDF congress made other important decisions too which indicated how far this alternative organization had developed. A national campaign was announced against black vigilante groups such as Chief Buthelezi's Inkatha, which were being used extensively against UDF both in single incidents, such as murders of key UDF activists, and in street warfare, assisting the security forces to break UDF-organized resistance to mass removals to Bantustans. The congress also for the first time emphasized some relevant developments beyond South Africa itself, indicating growing political maturity and ambitions for an international profile. The meeting both condemned Malawi, Lesotho and Swaziland for their links with Pretoria, and pledged to raise UDF members' level of knowledge about the achievement and sacrifices of Front-line States such as Angola, Mozambique, Tanzania, Zambia and others directly targeted by South Africa. There were also new international connections.

The UDF announced support for nuclear disarmament and world peace movements which they linked to the international forces most supportive of the anti-apartheid struggle. The UDF also pledged to campaign for acceptance of the Geneva Convention, which South Africa has always refused to recognize with the result that captured ANC guerrillas are still being executed. In addition, the meeting warned its members for the first time about US and other Western attempts to use funding of UDF affiliates to gain long-term influence within the opposition movement.

These congresses were evidence of a certain sophistication and capacity for underground organization; this, together with their open endorsement of the ANC leaders' opposition to the minority regime, allowed the ANC, in mid-1987, to pose more clearly than ever before its open challenge to the legitimacy of the ruling party. The whites-only election of May 1987 had shown that the ANC leadership, rather than the parliamentary opposition from right or left, was the main target of President Botha's National Party. The extra-parliamentary opposition of the UDF in the country, and of the ANC outside, had entered a new phase of potential strength. Pretoria's Western allies chose to underestimate this in a calculated attempt to buy yet more time; they tried to use the ever-increasing weakness of the Front-line States to put pressure on the ANC to call off the armed struggle and negotiate with Pretoria.

In a speech in London in May 1987 ANC President Oliver Tambo, in a remarkable display of confidence in the opposition organization within the country and in its loyalty to the exiled ANC's leadership, altered the terms of the cultural and academic boycott of South Africa which, begun in the 1950s, had done much to isolate the regime from the international community. President Tambo said that the new democratic structures which had grown up in South Africa in every field and community, in local and regional organizations of the UDF, should now be supported by the international community.

As in almost every other field of human endeavour in South Africa there has emerged a definable alternative democratic culture – the people's culture permeated with and giving expression to the deepest aspirations of our people in struggle, immersed in democratic and enduring human values. This is a development taking place within the context of the emergent alternative democratic power whose duty is to draw on the academic and cultural resources and heritage of the world community to advance the democratic perspective in our country . . .

As in politics, trade unionism, education, sport, religion, and many other fields, these developments at the cultural level both contributed to and are part of the emergent alternative democratic power at whose head stands the ANC. This means that the ANC, the broad democratic movement in its various formations with South Africa, and the international solidarity movement, need to act together.

The speech was the open recognition of a slow process of building organizational contacts outside the country which had been hesitantly begun on many fronts by the UDF.

In response to the unmistakeable evidence of the organizational capacity of the UDF, state-sponsored vigilante activity against its members increased dramatically in late 1987 and 1988, especially using Chief Buthelezi's Inkatha in Natal. And in February 1988 Pretoria went all out to clamp down on UDF and 17 of its affiliates, such as SAYCO, by introducing stringent new regulations which effectively banned all their activities. COSATU too was prohibited from all but strictly trade-union work.

The 1987 shift in the ANC boycott policy was, too, a recognition of how active the US in particular had become in forging links with a wide gamut of South African organizations and individuals opposed to the government, but equally opposed to the UDF and the ANC. The weaker and less socialist-orientated organizations were systematically promoted by the US, especially in the case of the Pan-African Congress. Scholarships, travel grants and conference tickets in significant numbers were given to people from the PAC, Black Consciousness and Chief Buthelezi's Inkatha. The promotion of divisive far-left splinter groups was also a CIA tactic. In both Western Europe and the United States a significant dent was made in the previous period's acceptance of the ANC as the only, or at least the leading, actor in the South African civil war. Confusion over which of the avowed 'brother enemies' to support was extensively sown in Africa by the United States directly and indirectly. This was not a new campaign and was able to build on previous initiatives, such as the visit to Nigeria in 1977 of Chief Buthelezi, at the invitation of the then Director-General of the Nigerian Institute of International Affairs, Bolaji Akinyemi. An influential Nigerian network, many of whose members were linked to the Carter White House, had, in the aftermath of the Soweto uprising, taken a number of South African youths for military training and education in Nigeria, with the aim of producing a third force – not a socialist one – in South African politics. Once Mr Akinyemi became Nigerian Foreign Minister the search for such a third force was an important element in the behind-the-scenes African and US promotion of PAC, Black Consciousness and Chief Buthelezi.

PAC, which had been virtually dormant inside South Africa for years and rent with murderous in-fighting in exile, began by the 1980s to be particularly heavily promoted by the US in many fora outside South Africa. The OAU had left the door open for just such an initiative by keeping both South African organizations within the OAU liberation committee in Dar Es Salaam. Both received equal funds from the OAU although there were few illusions that PAC's funds were being used for fighting. A drug-selling scandal involving PAC officials in Zimbabwe was hushed up, for instance. Mainly for generous sentimental reasons no one in Africa had ever wanted to take the initiative to expel a South African group of supposed freedom fighters from the continent's historic liberation committee, however discredited or virtually forgotten it had become at home. Inevitably, given the emergence of civil war inside South Africa, PAC began to claim responsibility from outside for some of the military actions inside the country, as a way of staking a claim to the future. They claimed too that, in contrast to the ANC's dispersal in bases in the Front-line States, PAC was deeply embedded within South Africa itself. These claims were largely contradicted by organized labour and community organizations, who worked with newly infiltrated ANC military and political cadres and saw no evidence of PAC organization within the townships.

From having little in the way of political profile internationally any more than at home, PAC began, as the struggle deepened, conveniently to articulate Washington's own thinking on the future direction of the regional conflicts. PAC was strongly anti-communist and openly critical not only of the ANC but of some of the Front-line States, most notably Angola and to a lesser extent Mozambique, for having, PAC claimed, allowed an East–West dimension to enter the regional struggle against apartheid. PAC also criticized the SWAPO leadership for having its headquarters outside the country (SWAPO's provisional headquarters were in Luanda but the organization retained Windhoek, the Namibian capital, as its technical headquarters throughout the war). PAC also promoted a SWAPO compromise with the internal government installed by South Africa. For years the South African and the US officials had been trying unsuccessfully to persuade SWAPO's President Sam Nujoma to agree to this proposition, and, equally unsuccessfully, to get others in the region to back it.

With a remarkable touch for far-reaching propaganda effect PAC leader Johnson Mlambo took advantage of the winds of change of the Gorbachev era to launch the idea (*Le Monde*, 12 June 1987) that the longstanding support of the Soviet Union to the ANC was under review. He claimed that a prudent shift of position by the Soviet leadership was being considered: 'so as not to repeat the unhappy experience of Zimbabwe where the Kremlin supported Joshua Nkomo against Robert Mugabe, they want now to be neutral between the different liberation movements.' Mr Mlambo's interview in Dar Es Salaam was intended as a pre-emptive strike against an impending move against the PAC within the OAU. The anti-communist line did in fact gain PAC the support of Libya and Iran. PAC was also supported by the African regimes with a historical anti-socialist bias or internal reasons to fear the example of a successful alternative left-wing government. For this is what the ANC/UDF would be, were it to come to power in Africa's most highly capitalized country and the continent's potential leader.

While this confused and confusing manoeuvring for influence outside the country continued, the ANC made considerable advances within South Africa. Its military presence was growing and, on the symbolic level, ANC colours at funerals and the veneration of leaders such as Mandela, Tambo and

Slovo were ubiquitous. At the same time, international opinion increasingly favoured the ANC's long-standing demand for economic sanctions against South Africa. In 1987 Scandinavia and even the EEC instituted mild sanctions, an unthinkable step only a year before. Customer and shareholder opinion in the banking community and in powerful transnationals was so overwhelmingly in favour of sanctions that one multinational after another removed its capital from South Africa – 200 companies by 1989. However an estimated half of those companies who did so maintained their profits through licensing arrangements.

The US government, meanwhile, co-ordinated approaches to and within Africa and especially the Front-line States, with the same goal as ever of weakening the nationalist movement in South Africa itself and the region in general. One of the propaganda cards played most frequently and most audaciously was Jonas Savimbi. The UNITA leader, as so often, spoke for Washington first and Pretoria second when he appeared in Johannesburg at a meeting of businessmen, shortly after the 1987 white election. In his most highly publicized visit to his long-time backers in South Africa Mr Savimbi praised President Botha for the changes he had initiated in the apartheid system. Without mentioning the ANC by name, he criticized those black leaders who refused to negotiate with Pretoria. 'President Botha needs support now,' Mr Savimbi declared. He was warmly welcomed by Foreign Minister R. F. Botha, who said that the future battle in South Africa would have nothing to do with colour but would develop along ideological lines. It was an echo of Savimbi's old slogans slung in banners from the trees at Jamba: 'Russian, Czechs, Cubans, go home, UNITA key to Angola, Angola key to Africa, Africa key to the West.'

Anti-communism had by 1987 given US and South African policy some legitimacy internationally so that a massive new South African ground invasion sweeping hundreds of miles into Angola made little stir. South Africa made no attempt to deny the October fighting they had done for Savimbi; at Mavinga they had turned back an Angolan government column, which suffered very heavy losses. Just two years before at Mavinga, where the Angolan army was making a push for Savimbi's headquarters at Jamba, the South Africans had been content to intervene mainly with air power. By 1987 Savimbi was able to use the US Stinger missiles given him by the Reagan administration after his visit to Washington the previous year. The missiles forced the Angolan Air Force to fly too high for effective protection of the ground troops. Meanwhile the US Senate, sufficiently unmoved by the South African aggression, or sufficiently intimidated by the anti-communist mood in Washington, had approved resolutions banning trade with the Angolan government and putting at risk the continuation of Chevron's important oil business in Angola's Cabinda province. (In May 1985 South Africa had made a different kind of attempt to dissuade US oil companies from doing business with Angola. A South African Army Captain, Wynand Du Toit, was captured in Cabinda, with his face blackened and a bag of UNITA pamphlets, trying to blow up the installations.)

When Mr Savimbi was not being shown off to the Western press in Johannesburg he was having Western reporters flown into Jamba and Mavinga for interviews and press conferences. His, and UNITA's international profile were deliberately raised, as part of the tide of pressure for conciliation being mounted on the Angolans and across the region including within South Africa itself.

The OAU chairman in 1986–7, Colonel Denis Sassou Nguesso of Congo, was one of the key protagonists of conciliation then demanded by the United States on many fronts. For instance, he visited Morocco, although the country was no longer a member of the OAU. It was in fact in continuing and flagrant violation of the continental organization's resolutions, which demanded a ceasefire with Polisario and a UN-sponsored referendum in the Western Sahara. He was also active behind the scenes in renewed US attempts to get the MPLA into dialogue with Washington again in spite of the Reagan administration's now open support for Savimbi. After a visit to Washington President Sassou Nguesso hosted a meeting in Brazzaville in mid-1987, which reopened talks between Chester Crocker, for the US, and the Angolan Interior Minister, Manuel 'Kito' Rodrigues.

Further, as though to emphasize the advisability of conciliation, a new and threatening military factor emerged at almost
the same time from Zaïre. The American government was
revealed to have several times carried out joint exercises with
the Zaïre army and to be planning a major refit of the massive
Kamina airbase in Shaba province. In early 1987 the Defense
Department in Washington asked the Reagan administration
to negotiate a formal access agreement to the run-down base;
this would allow the unpublicized joint US–Zaïrean troop
exercises of previous years to develop into a wider ranging
collaboration. A modest $2 million was initially set aside by
the Pentagon for this.

In the run-up to Angolan independence Kamina had been
the launching pad for the 1975 US-backed offensive of Holden
Roberto's FNLA and its British and American mercenaries
against the MPLA from the north while the South Africans
invaded from the south. Earlier, Kamina, the most strategic
and ambitious military base in Central Africa, had been
conceived as a possible NATO base, in case the Katanga
secessionists and their West European backers had succeeded
in splitting the Congo. Built by the Belgians in the mid-1950s,
well before the independence of their colony was envisaged,
Kamina is near the rail link to Zambia and is served by two
10,000 foot runways, large enough to take the US air force's
largest plane, the C5A transport. Among Kamina's facilities is
a 750-bed hospital, a cinema and a substantial stock of storage
space and housing. US forces used Kamina during the missionary hostage crisis in Kisangani (then Stanleyville) in 1964
when Belgian paratroopers were dropped from US planes in a
rescue operation. Again, in 1977 and 1978, US military forces
used Kamina to support the French, Belgian and Moroccan
troops airlifted in to defeat the two Shaba rebellions against
President Mobutu.

However, after Angolan independence the Clark amendment of 1976 prohibited military aid to the MPLA's opponents,
and the use of Kamina against Angola appeared to have
stopped, at least for a while. For years nothing was heard of
the remote Zaïrean base, but evidence of its use in support of
UNITA began to leak out during the mid-1980s. Saudi Arabian

as well as US planes were spotted landing shipments of arms for UNITA in southern Zaïre. They were not isolated incidents but part of an elaborate network, using an old connection. Saudi Arabia had financed the Moroccan part of the emergency military rescue mission for President Mobutu in 1977. Saudi financial support too for much of the training of Savimbi's men in Morocco was a fairly well-known part of their financial aid to the Moroccan armed forces. But few people knew that for years, deep in the Zaïrean bush, US engineers had periodically appeared at dusk to lay portable strip lighting along Kamina's runways for military supply planes for UNITA. The Saudi planes were just one example of an important, through normally invisible, thread in Washington's Africa policy.

The great size of Zaïre, its lack of internal democracy or of any but the rarest visiting Western journalist, and the US and Belgian complicity which had allowed President Mobutu to amass a personal fortune as large as the national debt in Western banks outside his country, had made the huge Central African nation the perfect base for secret operations. The US was able to use not only Saudi Arabia as the financier or facilitator of some of these activities but also Israel. Zaïre was one of the few African countries to reopen diplomatic links with Israel after more than a decade of isolation of the Zionist state by almost all members of the OAU.

Discreet Israeli liaison, and in some cases military supply lines, were established in Zaïre for use, or possible use, on a wider African canvas than even southern Africa. Using Zaïre and Kenya the Israelis had access to the whole region. Active CIA conduits into civil wars in southern Sudan and Uganda were in place in 1985–6 for instance. Dr John Garang's Sudan People's Liberation Army (SPLA), fighting the Khartoum government led by Prime Minister Sadiq el Mahdi, was primarily supported by the Ethiopian government. The Ethiopians hoped to use their patronage of the southern rebellion as a lever to persuade the Sudanese government to cut transit and other facilities to the Eritrean and Tigrean guerrilla movements; these were fighting the Derg in Addis Ababa for independence or at least autonomy. The Derg's contact with

Garang's rebellion was to turn out to be a useful vindication of Washington's policy of targeting individuals within progressive governments. A top government official in Addis Ababa, Major Dawit Wolde Giorgis, was an Israeli-trained parachute officer whose previous experience in southern Sudan was as the Israeli link and military trainer to the earlier southern Sudanese rebellion, the Anyanya. From being Colonel Mengistu's trusted liaison with Garang, through a period where Garang made some strange and destructive decisions which aborted peace talks with Khartoum, Major Dawit defected to Washington in 1985. The SPLA leader, educated at universities in Tanzania and the United States, enjoyed the reputation of having forged a left-wing movement. In fact the SPLA had little coherent ideology, but was more of a peasant movement based on ethnic alliances. In addition, the SPLA was supported by some opportunist individuals who had opposed President Nimeiri in his last period: this included former Foreign Minister Mansour Khalid, architect of many of President Nimeiri's business ventures in his pro-American phase. CIA links through Zaïre and Kenya helped to maintain the increasingly confused southern rebellion to an extent which prevented the post-Nimeiri nationalist regime of Sadiq el Mahdi from consolidating and rebuilding the shattered Sudanese economy. The draining of this former bread basket of the Arab world became as inexorable as, say, that of Angola's oil-based economy. Sudan's southern neighbour Uganda suffered too from the lawless no-go areas along the border with Sudan; it provided sanctuaries for armed groups bent on a destabilizing northern war which sapped the energy and legitimacy of the nationalist government of President Yoweri Museveni. When the strange war of witchdoctors and bandits spread to the east of Uganda, supported by supplies coming through Kenya no one in the region was surprised.

After the overthrow of the second regime of Milton Obote by a section of his own military in July 1985 the shaky Okello regime which replaced it was propped up indirectly by the US and other Western powers; they were interested in seeing another pliable government come to power in Uganda – strategically important because of its borders with Kenya,

Sudan and Zaïre. It was particularly Kenya (which, during the Reagan administration, became more important to the US when a military facilities agreement was signed by President Daniel Arap Moi in 1981) which provided regional diplomatic support to the barely credible military junta headed by General Tito Okello, then opposing Yoweri Museveni's National Resistance Army. The US was instrumental in arms shipments from Egypt and Western Europe, paid for by Saudi Arabia, which were brought in for Okello's army during the autumn, while inconclusive peace talks with Museveni were spun out in Kenya under the chairmanship of President Daniel Arap Moi. In the final days of the Okello regime, with many of its own soldiers defecting to the NRA, Museveni was invited to Washington by the Reagan administration. While he was supposed to be *en route* a secret plan which had been devised by the US was to be put into action. The Americans had organized that Israeli crack troops be flown in from Zaïre to hold the airport and key places in Kampala, in exchange for diplomatic recognition of Israel by the Okello regime. The plan failed because Museveni, instead of travelling to Washington himself, sent his delegation on ahead, and stayed in Uganda to co-ordinate the attack on Kampala that brought him to power in January 1986. The incident illustrated the ruthless and illegal character of US foreign policy at this time, which would be further revealed in other regions of the White House's private wars and deals conducted by Colonel Oliver North and the CIA chief William Casey.

When the Iran/'contra' scandal began to unravel in late 1986 it included a shadowy Zaïre/Angolan dimension. St Lucia Airlines, a tiny Caribbean-based airline, emerged as a secret conduit for deliveries of illegal arms shipments to Iran. Its flights to Israel and Tehran were not routinely logged, but classified by the US Air Force according to company officials. St Lucia planes, which regularly carried such cargo as chickens or beer from Belgium to Zaïre, also touched down at Kamina on several occasions in late 1986 when arms for UNITA were seen being unloaded; company officials, however, claimed that they were not arms but relief flights to Zaïre. At the same time another air transport company with longstanding links with the CIA – indeed actually owned by it from 1960 to 1973 – was working within Angola. Southern Air Transport of Miami was flying supply missions between Luanda and the north-eastern diamond mines, but its log books also showed flights to the important Angola base at Cuito Cuanavale on the Cuban-manned defence line across the south of the country, and, even more curiously, to Chitado, an airstrip on the Namibian border. Southern Air Transport had been flying military equipment and fuel to the most sensitive war areas in Angola. It is difficult to believe these flights were as casual or disinterested as they were claimed to have been. Southern Air Transport in fact had a special usefulness to the Angola military which was certainly not accidental. The company had only Lockheed L100 Hercules transport planes in Angola because the Reagan administration, from 1986, forbade the sale to the Angolans of heavy cargo aircraft.

Although Southern Air Transport had been sold by the CIA in 1973, it was still working for the Agency in 1986 in Nicaragua. In October of that year a C130 cargo plane was shot down by the Sandinistas while on a supply mission to the 'contras'. The plane's cargo handler, Eugene Hasenfus, was captured, tried and later released by the Nicaraguan government, but two crew members died. Both of them, Wallace Blaine Sawyer Jr and William Cooper, had been flying for Southern Air Transport in Angola only weeks before, and Mr Cooper, according to his associates, knew the country so well 'he could fly without a map'. The mysterious Southern Air Transport operations were an extricable part of the confused battles of carrots and sticks waged by Washington in Angola. They aptly symbolized the contradictory strands of American policy towards Angola, and the difficulty for such weakened governments to check the multiplicity of US methods of penetration, even into their own military. A light plane piloted by a US citizen, Joseph Frank Long, was shot down by the Angolan Air Force over the sensitive security area of Cahana in Southern Angola in April 1987; it was another example of the audacity of US actions in the region. Mr Long's claim to be a civilian who was delivering the single-engined Bonanza aircraft to South African Airways, but had strayed several hundred miles off course, was not easy to credit.

Angola officials were extremely concerned about the CIA's use of Kamina for supplying UNITA, and the potential threat implied by the US government's apparent readiness to sign an open agreement with President Mobutu for its upgrading and use by American troops. But President Dos Santos was preparing to join the IMF, and continuing his efforts to win better relations with Washington and hoping to head off Savimbi's rising support in the US. The Angolan leaders said little publicly. Only Sam Nujoma of SWAPO, among all the Front-line States' leaders, spoke out openly against an American military presence in or access to Kamina, which he said was a threat to the whole Southern and Central African region. In the aftermath of the US bombing of Libyan towns in mid-1986, as retribution for alleged terrororist attacks, Sam Nujoma drew a chilling parallel for the Front-line States which were constantly accused by South Africa of harbouring terrorists and had already suffered airstrikes from South Africa on that pretext. But in the atmosphere of confrontation with black African states which dominated the US Congress, if not US public opinion, in this period, the Front-line leadership chose to stay silent. The example of Savimbi's promotion and the legitimization of opposition was intimidating enough to discourage other governments from striking any public posture which could provoke the Reagan administration into openly or covertly promoting any of their own dissidents into a powerful political force. Both Mozambique and Zimbabwe were already threatened with just such an outcome.

No one wanted to attack Zaïre publicly either. Around the Zaïre government too a discreet battle for influence was underway by the Front-line States against the US and South Africa. In late 1986, just before the death of President Samora Machel, the Front-line States had started their own version of carrot and stick pressure against both Malawi's and Zaïre's role as proxies in the South African war against the region. The Front-line States were demanding nothing less than that their two neighbours change sides. But whereas in the east both Tanzania and Mozambique had been forthright, and had threatened President Hastings Banda of Malawi with a blockade of the railways in and out of his landlocked country, in the west Angola and Zambia took a softer line with President Mobutu. The Zaïrean President was of course less vulnerable to trade sanctions and, reflecting the strategic importance of Zaïre to the US, likely to be better protected by his powerful friends.

So, with the Angolans tactfully silent about Kamina and saying little openly either about repeated UNITA incursions from Zaïrean territory into Angola's Zaïre and Uige provinces in the northwest of the country, a new diplomatic battleground was prepared around the startling new possibility of reopening the long-paralysed Benguela railway. In 1980 a project to reopen the route was put to SADCC and the European community, without success. Now, the discussions, strongly encouraged by the Americans, notably Dr Chester Crocker, served many different, and conflicting, interests. In spite of US and British opposition to trade and other sanctions against South Africa the international climate was running strongly in favour of sanctions. Substantial international capital was thus for the first time beginning to be available for infrastructural projects, as alternatives to South African routes. The basic rehabilitation of Benguela, sabotaged repeatedly by UNITA was estimated to cost about $200 million. Reconstruction and modernization would take at least three years to complete.

The Benguela railway was built in 1920 by the British with minor Portuguese participation. Its 800 miles of track wound out from the Zambian and Zaïrean copper belts before slicing from east to west across Angola to the Atlantic port of Lobito, which handled the lucrative export of copper. But after Angolan independence in 1975 the Benguela railway was an almost constant target for sabotage by UNITA and by the South Africans, exactly as were the railways and pipeline from Zimbabwe, Zambia and Malawi to the Indian Ocean ports of Beira, Nacala and Maputo in Mozambique on the other side of the continent. As had happened in the cases of trade from Zimbabwe and Malawi, Zaïre's Shaba province copper output, and Zambia's production of copper, which should have gone on the Benguela trains to the Angolan port of Lobito, became instead gradually largely dependent on South African ports. The Chinese-built TanZam railway to Dar Es Salaam did offer Zambia one alternative and by the mid-1980s was increasingly being used.

By the mid-1980s the Benguela line was only running from Lobito as far as Huambo in Angola's Central Highlands, a quarter of the way down the line to the Zaïre border. Between Huambo and the eastern province of Moxico convoys of trains could run very irregularly, but beyond that, from Luena to the border town of Luau, the railway was virtually disused. In conjunction with the periodic sabotage of rail tracks or bridges by mines placed by UNITA, the movement's leader frequently used the railway for propaganda purposes. Savimbi frequently took Western journalists to film and photograph the railway, especially at the little halt of Muchango in central Angola where he himself had been brought up.

Savimbi was quick to reveal himself as an aspiring actor in any political scene which involved Benguela. Immediately after the Brazzaville meeting between Dr Crocker and Angola's Interior Minister, Manuel 'Kito' Rodrigues, a partial Frontline summit of Angola, Zambia, Mozambique and Zaïre on 16 April 1987 announced a decision in principle to reopen the line. From Washington, and then in well-attended briefings for journalists flown to Jamba, Savimbi laid down his conditions for the railway to operate. He demanded first the demilitarization of the line itself, which would mean it could not carry weapons or soldiers, and second a so-called security zone either side of the line. The Angolans had already declared, in the 16 April four-nation summit in Lusaka, that the international traffic on the railway would be only civilian in character. That clause in the Lusaka communiqué, although it predated Savimbi's demand, appeared to be a significant and inexplicable concession by the MPLA leadership. At the same time, and in clear contradiction of the anti-MPLA mood in Congress, the Reagan administration rumoured that US diplomatic recognition for the government of Luanda was under consideration with a visit to Luanda by Secretary of State George Schultz. The Benguela reopening saga thus apeared to be a fresh opportunity for a replay of Dr Crocker's constructive engagement, with reconciliation again being demanded by Washington.

As in every previous scene in the constructive engagement story regional gains – in this case improved international rail links, an influx of capital and reduced dependence of the region on South Africa – were to be set against internal concessions, this time by Angola making a deal with Savimbi which would finally lead to the withdrawal of Cuban trops.

The Zambian leader, Dr Kenneth Kaunda, a supporter of Savimbi in the days before the UNITA leader had entered his open alliance with the South Africans, was one of the advocates of Angolan concessions to US demands; he agreed even to the pull-back of Cuban troops if this was necessary in order to get the Benguela railway working again. The railway was a much-needed new means of access for landlocked Zambia. In addition any step towards lowering the profile of UNITA and even checking the war inside Angola for a while would be a much-needed breathing space in a tide of refugees and military dislocation in the west of the country. Besides, as home to the headquarters of the African National Congress in exile, Lusaka was conscious of its special vulnerability to direct South African attacks. One year after the May 1986 bombings by South Africa in which Zambia was hit, as were Botswana and Zimbabwe, it suffered a closely targeted South African attack on the border town of Livingston and four Zambian civilians were killed. The South Africans, in an attempt to justify this helicopter and motorcycle raid, claimed that it had killed 'five African National Congress terrorists'. The South African practice was to claim that their attacks were on ANC targets and to issue warnings that Front-line States such as Zambia were on the point of infiltrating ANC guerrillas into South Africa, and this created a climate of fear and destabilization which hit all the regional economies.

Zambia's own economic situation was by 1987 a microcosm of the whole continent's fragility and enforced deference to Western-led international financial institutions. Export revenues in Africa fell by 29 per cent in 1986 alone, mainly because of the catastrophic crash in prices of commodities such as copper, which had been Zambia's life blood, while cocoa and coffee slumped to such an extent that even the previously successful Ivory Coast suspended debt payments. The continent's debt burden was, by the mid-1980s, a clearly unpayable $218 billion – 75 per cent of it owed to Western governments. In Zambia the average income had dropped by two thirds in a decade, leaving the social fabric so precarious that little was needed to bring the government itself under threat. In such a context, the government's economic policies were, even more than usual, the key to its political survival. A political threat in Zambia came from two directions. Other Front-line States too suffered the same constraints on government policy. First there were Zambia's own businessmen, who opposed the government's policy of favouring the imposition of economic sanctions against South Africa. A group which shared the Western and South African line that sanctions would harm their own businesses were even at one point arrested in Lusaka and accused of plotting a military coup against the government with South African complicity. Second, at another level of society, in the wake of an IMF agreement which removed subsidies on basic foods, riots rocked northern copper belt towns and armed police opened fire, killing twelve workers. Zambia's President Kaunda then declared that the country would rescind its recently announced price increases and abrogate its IMF agreement; the conditions imposed, he said, were too harsh to be realistic and struck at the government's very legitimacy in the eyes of its own people.

In mid-1987 at a UN conference on Africa's economic crisis in Nigeria's new capital Abuja, Professor Adebayo Adedeji, speaking for the whole continent, asked rhetorically whether it was 'inevitable, or a *sine qua non*, for recovery to cut down in those areas where major advances were made in the post-independence era – health, education, infrastructural facilities or social overhead capital – in order to achieve a short-term turnaround of our economies'. The short answer, as every government minister in Africa knew by then, was yes. The loss of sovereignty to Western institutions, so often forecast by Nyerere, had already taken place and among the African states drawn into these new and unequal relationships with the

West were Angola and Mozambique – formerly Marxist–Leninist states by self-definition.

But while South Africa's neighbours sought their various sad compromises to survive so that the next generation might fight and win, it was the white regime in Pretoria which had the most desperate and deepening struggle for a future. As Sam Nujoma put it, they had become 'the hostages of Afrikaner history'.

Chapter 10

Bitter Peace

_____

In the first week of April 1989, as Namibia's long-delayed independence procedure from South Africa got under way, there were no celebrations in northern Namibia. Instead, the villagers mourned beside mass graves of naked young men, many of them executed at gunpoint by South African troops. With a deadly mixture of weakness and muddle, reminiscent of the Congo's decolonization tragedy, the United Nations, which took over responsibility for Namibia on 1 April 1989, presided over this massacre of Namibian nationalists by the occupying South African army. It was the tragically apt conclusion to years of international indifference to South Africa's economic exploitation and vicious repression of the continent's last colony, and, typical of the Alice-in-Wonderland perceptions which rule in relations between South Africa and its black neighbours, the Western press and the international community chose to blame the leaders of the nationalist movement, SWAPO, for the heaps of dead youths, the flattened huts and burnt kraals which were northern Namibia's first sight of independence.

For one group of sixty or so young SWAPO guerrillas, sitting at ease in the shade at midday, eating, and asking passers-by for water and for directions to the nearest United Nations position, 1 April was seen as the first day of peace. Okahenge, where the guerrillas were given water by a local man, Jekonia Ngenokesho, is twenty-five kilometres south of the Angolan border in the heart of the northern war zone, where SWAPO guerrillas had fought their low-level war of sabotage and ambush against South Africa's huge occupying army. That day, the South African security forces had, under UN Resolution 435 of 1978, been confined to barracks under UN supervision at 4 a.m., the guerrillas believed. Suddenly a line of Casspir armoured cars rumbled out of the bush and the guerrillas told Jekonia Ngenokesho and his brother to run for their lives.

The guerrillas themselves were sitting targets for the first stage of South Africa's carefully laid ambush, which aimed to achieve overnight what Pretoria had not managed in two decades of war – the annihilation of SWAPO as a military force. This would mean that if the liberation movement were to win the UN-supervised election in November 1989 it would come to power crippled by having no army – an event unprecedented after any armed struggle in Africa. The local pastor from the nearby town of Endola arrived at the battle-site early next morning to find a heap of thirty-three bodies, some in uniform, some naked. All day he stayed with the dead men waiting for the same United Nations monitoring force that they, too, had waited for in vain. Meanwhile, throughout the day, battles had raged at thirty places along the northern border, and several hundred other SWAPO guerrillas crossed the border from Angola to aid those ambushed. Sixty major battles were recorded in the next few days.

The flawed start to Namibia's independence was the culmination of dramatic shifts in power-relations in the whole Southern African region during 1988, and came against the backdrop of geo-political change which put President Mikhail Gorbachev's bid for disarmament and *détente* with the United States at the top of the Soviet Union's foreign policy agenda. From the moment the Soviet Union announced its troop withdrawal from Afghanistan on terms which would allow continued military support by the US, as well as the continued availability of Pakistan's intelligence services, to the Mujahideen guerrillas against the Afghan government, a pattern for the settlement of regional conflicts was born. Despite the often-repeated Soviet assurances that there were no losers in the peace process, there were, inevitably, winners and losers in all the regional settlements. American diplomacy ensured that their prime clients were not the losers anywhere. The mass graves in northern

Namibia in early April were a crude reminder of the price that losers should expect to pay, although for the young men relaxing in northern Namibia in the mid-morning of 1 April, it was not a price they had expected. The fact that South Africa had been able to keep SWAPO outside all the long negotiations leading to the settlement, and had never signed a ceasefire with the independence movement, was an ominous indication of Pretoria's continuing ability to call the shots – literally.

In late 1987, and 1988, there were also other dynamics towards a new peace bid in Southern Africa than the superpowers' wish for an end to regional conflicts. On 16 November 1987 the Central Committee of the Cuban Communist Party decided to reinforce its troops in Angola to counter a massive new South African build-up of infrastructure and logistics in northern Namibia, which had begun in March 1987 in preparation for the most ambitious offensive since the one on the brink of Angola's independence in 1975.

The Cubans had decided during 1987 that the deepening social, political and military crisis in South Africa, the international mood favouring regional *détente*, and the passionate desire of the outgoing Reagan administration to claim credit for a Cuban withdrawal, provided the opportunity for the allied forces in Angola, suitably strengthened with some of Havana's finest military cadres, to make a sudden push for a precise objective – Namibia's independence.

It was a dramatic shift of vision from President Fidel Castro's defiant pronouncement at the Non-Aligned Movement summit in Harare in the summer of 1986 that Cuba would 'remain in Angola until the end of apartheid'. A year later, the Cubans believed that the independence of Namibia under UN Resolution 435 need no longer wait for the end of apartheid but could, in fact, be a significant step towards it. It was a high-risk decision, not least because the Angolan military were in serious trouble near the south-eastern town of Cuito Cuanavale after an advance which was to be criticized publicly by Castro. The South African offensive, which had begun earlier in the year, aimed at the capture of Cuito Cuanavale as the new strategic base for Pretoria's allies in UNITA to advance into central Angola and increase their

pressure on the Angolan government for a political settlement. Throughout much of Angola, UNITA forces about
20,000-strong – well-equipped by South Africa, funded by the
US, increasingly trained in Morocco and supported by Israeli-
aided facilities in Zaïre – were attacking new target areas,
especially in the north. Meanwhile, logistical failures meant
that government troops were running short of food and
equipment, and morale was low.

But from January 1988 the massive Cuban reinforcement,
under the same generals who had been the heroes of the first
Cuban offensive against the South Africans in 1975, changed
the picture. The Cubans, for the first time since they repelled
the South African invasion of 1975, moved on to the offensive
and swept south and east to meet the South Africans head-on
at Cuito Cuanavale. The battle for Cuito raged through late
February 1988 until the end of March, when the South African
troops were forced to withdraw southwards by the combined
forces of Angolan, Cuban and SWAPO troops. For the first
time, SWAPO forces were openly fighting inside Angola – a
symbolic underlining by all parties of the changed and inter-
linked nature of the wars for Angolan sovereignty and
Namibian independence. During the fighting, both sides took
very heavy casualties. Among the South African soldiers who
died were nineteen-year-old white conscripts whose deaths
rebounded back into the white suburbs and colleges of South
Africa and rendered the deep invasion into Angola politically
untenable.

Compounding the military crisis exacerbated by the loss of
air superiority to the Angolan and Cuban forces and the
out-classing of South Africa's much-vaunted weaponry from
its own state manufacturing company, Armscor, a social crisis
surfaced in South Africa when 143 white youths from the End
Conscription Campaign publicly refused to do their National
Service and fight in Angola and Namibia. The ECC, later to be
banned by Pretoria, suffered a dirty tricks campaign, from the
regime, which was serious enough for the ECC to bring the
military to court and have an injunction granted against
further harassment. The first of the ECC's 143 to be tried in
court, David Bruce, was given a six-year sentence in an

attempt to deter what looked like the beginning of a major trend of white dissent.

It was against this background that Pretoria went to the conference table in a London hotel in May 1988, using consummate skill in public relations to obscure the retreat of its defeated army inside Angola. That London meeting also served as an occasion to present a new reasonable image of South Africa, ready and willing to grant Namibia independence at last under the terms of the ten-year-old Resolution 435.

This was to be the linchpin of a far-reaching campaign by Pretoria to win international respectability for a 'reformed' apartheid regime – a campaign which, over the next six months, paid off with visits by the South African leadership to six black African capitals never before (with the exception of Blantyre) prepared to receive them. In a series of negotiations in Brazzaville, Cairo, Geneva and New York, South Africa presented itself as a rational, viable political interlocutor in state-to-state relations. In this same period the Pope and UN Secretary General Perez de Cuellar both visited South Africa, and President Botha skilfully capitalized on the funeral of his close friend, Franz-Joseph Strauss, to visit the all-important bankers of Switzerland, before going on to Portugal and the Ivory Coast. The National Party was pushing back the threat of isolation, and of international economic sanctions.

The Namibian independence process and the courting of black Africa marked the beginning of a new phase in the South African government's strategy of survival. Eight years of the American policy of 'constructive engagement' under President Reagan, and little prospect of any real change under a US President who had been head of the CIA during one of its most active periods in southern Africa, had given Pretoria the confidence to re-examine its tactics. Besides, the threat of 'total onslaught' on South Africa by communist forces, for so long Pretoria's justification for repression at home and destabilization of its neighbours, was clearly no longer tenable. To meet the new geo-political situation created by Moscow's *perestroika*, and in rising to the challenge of a hostile US

Congress's demands for increased economic sanctions, Pretoria worked hard both on its high-profile foreign policy and on the image of internal reform, with even National Party spokesmen declaring that apartheid was on the way out.

However, continuing Draconian press censorship and the routine extension, on 16 July 1989, of the State of Emergency for the third time, obscured the extent of internal repression. The black leadership said repeatedly that repression was more intense in the late 1980s than in the 1960s – a period that witnessed the initial banning of the ANC, the Rivonia Trial, and the imprisonment of Nelson Mandela.

Part of the government's new strategy was to make apparent concessions to international opinion in the most important, symbolic cases in the black community. In what appeared to be a step-by-step liberation, the ANC leader, Nelson Mandela, symbol above all others of the black nationalist movement, was freed from Pollsmoor prison, first into a luxury clinic where he was treated for tuberculosis, and then into a bungalow in the grounds of Victor Verster prison where the authorities offered him unrestricted visits from his family (a personal concession which he refused to accept). Also, the Sharpeville Six, whose conviction on murder charges on the basis of 'common purpose' became an international *cause célèbre* in 1988, had their death sentences commuted at the last moment. Executions of less publicized cases continued nevertheless and there were 117 hangings in 1988 and 300 people on Death Row in mid-1989. The highly publicized reprieve also effectively signalled to the outside world that Pretoria was ready to ignore the demands of its own far-right extremists for no concessions either to international opinion or to the black majority in the country. In the same mood, the government used the familiar tactic of the banning of an organization, but for the first time against a white group, the neo-Nazi Blanke Bevrydigingsbeweging (BBB) or White Liberation Front. The BBB had campaigned for all Jews to be expelled from South Africa and for all blacks to be forcibly removed to black homelands. The banning came in the wake of a massacre by a crazed Afrikaner gunman on the streets of Pretoria's Barend Strydom; he was a member not of BBB but of the larger and better known extremist organization, the Afrikan Weerstande Beweging (AWB). He left six blacks dead and fifteen wounded. The leader of the BBB, Johan Schabort, became the first right-wing Afrikaner to be served with the banning orders so familiar to black activists.

The banning and restricting of organizations and individuals continued as one of the government's key strategies in trying to re-establish control of the black townships. This had been almost lost during the uprisings of 1984–5 which accompanied the formation of the United Democratic Front and the creation of a network of organizations opposed to the new constitution and tri-cameral parliament of 1984. Here too the government's sophisticated two-track strategy of mollifying international opinion by making apparent concessions can be seen in practice. For instance, the release in December 1988 of the detained editor of the *New Nation*, Zwelakhe Sisulu, who had been the subject of a huge international campaign, was welcomed internationally, but it was accompanied by conditions described by his lawyer as 'worse than prison'.

In early 1989 several hundred detainees, many of whom had been in prison since the first State of Emergency in 1986, went on hunger strikes in prisons across the country. The vast majority of those released as a result – about 500 – were restricted, like Zwelakhe Sisulu, by conditions which prevented them from doing their jobs. They were required to report twice a day to a police station often many miles from their homes, they were subjected to house arrest every evening, and prohibitions were placed on the number of people they could meet. For several of them, the predictability of their movements as a result of these conditions was a serious security risk and ex-detainees were ambushed or attacked at home. Among the detainees released then (or in some cases earlier) and restricted, were the elderly ANC leader Govan Mbeki, leaders of the UDF Christmas Tinto and Trevor Manuel, Eric Molobi of the National Education Crisis Committee, lawyers Azhar Cachalia and Yunis Mohamed, and law lecturer Raymond Suttner (forbidden to enter a university). Once released from detention, however, they were soon forgotten by the international community and pressure on the government was relaxed. The press restrictions, too, helped the government to keep such people and organizations, and the political option they represented, invisible. In 1988 alone, thirty-two anti-apartheid organizations, including the UDF, were banned.

Terrorist attacks on these organizations included the bombing, in September 1988, of Khotso House, the South African Council of Churches' Johannesburg headquarters, which virtually gutted the building and destroyed the offices of several anti-apartheid groups at one stroke. In the fifteen months before that blast no less than fourteen bombing and arson attacks took place on similar targets. The trade union federation, COSATU, saw its eleven-storey head office rendered uninhabitable by a bomb attack in May 1987. Throughout the following months a spate of fire-bombings, break-ins and lootings of union premises took place, and book publishers such as Ravan Press and newspapers such as *The Namibian* also received the same disabling treatment.

The South African State authorities continued their traditional tactics of targeting individuals, often going to great lengths to do so. The academic, David Webster (a British passport holder), who maintained support for detainees and their families with modest tea parties after the Detainee Parents Support Committee was banned, was assassinated outside his home, the sixtieth anti-apartheid activist similarly murdered inside the country. The lawyer, Yunis Mohamed, after surprising two security police officers engaged in a torchlight search of his papers in the office of the EEC-supported Kaghiso Trust, received death threats, including a condolence notice for his family placed in a newspaper. Mulana Faried Esack of the Call of Islam, after becoming one of the best-known spokesmen for the anti-apartheid movement across the world, was deprived of his passport after a harassment campaign which included the distribution of thousands of leaflets either attacking him personally, or purporting to be from the Call of Islam urging people to co-operate in the municipal elections of late 1988 which were boycotted by the majority of the black community. The Reverend Frank Chikane, Secretary General of the South African Council of

Churches, suffered a near fatal poisoning through a substance placed in his clothes during a visit to Namibia. He was hospitalized four times during a visit to the United States before US doctors were able to identify the poison.

When trade unionist Jabu Ndlovu died in the early hours of 1 June 1989 she was the 1,300th person to die violently in Pietermaritsburg in less than two years. She died after an attack on her house in which it was burned to the ground and her husband and daughter were killed. Behind Jabu Ndlovu's death was, almost certainly, her appearance at a Johannesburg press conference on behalf of COSATU, where very serious allegations were made about co-operation between Thulani Ngcobo, one of Natal's warlords, and the police.

Another aspect of the re-establishing of government control of the townships since the mid-1980s was the encouragement of vigilantes. The so-called 'black on black' violence which characterized Natal in particular in the three years before Jabu Ndlovu's death, was the most vicious manifestation of a government policy which replaced the white policing of townships of the years 1984–5. Besides the 1,300 killed, unknown tens of thousands of people were displaced and made internal refugees in conditions of civil war. Legal affidavits and court interdictions, accumulated by civil rights lawyers, demonstrated again and again the links between vigilante killings, led by Inkatha warlords, and the police. Western governments' support for Chief Buthelezi's Inkatha movement appeared unshaken by these legal revelations. By being vociferously opposed to Western economic sanctions against South Africa, Buthelezi could count on powerful Western voices speaking up to keep him in a political field where, increasingly since 1984, he had in fact lost a large part of his constituency.

Natal was one microcosm of what happened in many parts of South Africa. Another was the destruction in 1986 of the Crossroads squatter settlement of 30,000 people by vigilantes acting in concert with the security forces. The state had succeeded in dividing black communities, co-opting a section of the leadership opposed to the broad front anti-apartheid movement led by the UDF, and arming and supporting that leadership in a deadly military campaign against grassroots organizations opposed to the state strategy of the reform of apartheid.

The use of the judiciary against opponents of apartheid, and in particular against office bearers in the mass anti-apartheid organizations, was another strand of the same strategy. Late in 1988, in the landmark two-year-long Delmas trial, the UDF's leading officials, Popo Molefe, Patrick 'Terror' Lekota and Moss Chikane, were convicted of treason. The judge in their case accepted the state's submission that the UDF under their leadership was working for 'materially the same' policies as the ANC. This trial marked the effective criminalization of all opposition to government policies.

Behind all these government tactics lay the bitter struggle for political authority in the black community between the crippled organizations of the mass democratic movement and the South African government's Joint Management Centres which began upgrading black townships while breaking rent strikes and consumer boycotts.

The municipal elections of October 1988 provided one measure of the government's failure to impose its authority. In two Natal constituencies, Itsokolele and Msingisi, there were, respectively, only seven and eleven voters. Elsewhere candidates were scarce – 8 per cent of seats had no candidates, and in 43 per cent only one. If those living in the bantustans are included in the 40 million black population of South Africa, less than 10 per cent of blacks cast a vote despite the immense efforts of the government to encourage participation by advertising campaigns and by a system of prior-voting which brought out a number of elderly voters apparently convinced their pension depended on going to the polls.

To much of the black community electoral politics looked a pale sideshow beside the political struggle to keep banned organizations alive and the escalating urban guerrilla activities from the ANC's armed wing, Umkhonto we Siswe. In 1988 police figures for guerrilla attacks, which usually minimize incidents, were 291, compared with 234 the previous year. Trials throughout 1988–9 highlighted the growth of the armed struggle into a vast underground network in black and white communities, stretching from universities to townships.

Routine use of brutal torture by the security forces ensured that ANC cells were repeatedly broken. But a feature of trials such as that of ANC Commander Ashley Forbes in 1988, was that in prison the ANC cell reconstituted itself and the defendants came to court as a disciplined military group. And in the second landmark Delmas trial, of three ANC guerrillas in late 1988, the defendants came to court in military uniform and refused to plead in the civilian court.

The pattern of repression at home and diplomacy abroad reflected the belief of Pretoria and its allies that the outcome in the Namibia negotiations was critical to the future of South Africa. Would the negotiations which began in London in May 1988 ensure for Pretoria the economic and political dominance of the region which she had fought for in so many ways since the independence of Angola and Mozambique in 1975?

South Africa's defeat at Cuito Cuanavale weighted the military balance of power against Pretoria, but it did not take the strategic advantage away from the South African government. Throughout 1988 both sides threw all their weight into both military and diplomatic battles.

After the South Africans began to fall back from Cuito Cuanavale the combined Angolan/Cuban and SWAPO forces pushed south across a broad front into the *de facto* no-go area in Cunene province on the border with Namibia. After several heavy engagements most of the South African forces, together with the Namibian black conscript units, some of whom were fighting in UNITA uniforms, retreated over the border into Namibia. Cuban engineering units working round the clock under floodlights rapidly put in place anti-aircraft weapons to protect the new forward air-strips for southern Angola at Cahama and Xandongo, hamlets wrenched back from South African control. By June the South African generals knew that their remaining forces inside Angola were not only beaten but trapped, but, far from suing for peace, they called a meeting in the Congolese capital Brazzaville and attempted to persuade the Angolans into a bi-lateral negotiation, dropping Namibia from the deal and exchanging an SADF retreat from Angola for a Cuban withdrawal.

For the first time the informal proposal surfaced that ANC bases would have to be removed from Angola in return for a cessation of SADF support for UNITA. This proposal introduced a new element to the US 'linkage' of Namibian independence to the withdrawal of Cuban troops from Angola, an idea strongly opposed by the Angolans in the different climate of the early 1980s, but which could no longer be realistically resisted in the international mood of conciliation eight years on. This second 'linkage', of the ANC to UNITA, was an indication of just how effective a negotiating weapon Jonas Savimbi had been for the South Africans through the long destructive war he had waged as their proxy.

Continuing US military and political support for Savimbi was underlined by his visit to Washington during the negotiations, and by joint US and Zaïrean military manoeuvres in May which served to equip UNITA's northern bases inside Zaïre for their eventual expanded use if Namibian independence did force UNITA out of its Jamba base in southern Angola.

But Angola in 1988 was not Mozambique in 1984, and Pretoria was not able to turn the quadripartite negotiations into the diplomatic triumph of another Nkomati non-aggression pact. The South Africans made one further attempt, in Cairo, to play the dominant role, demanding a Cuban pull-out over the same seven-month period as UN Resolution 435 provided for the South African withdrawal from Namibia. This proposal nearly scuttled the talks and the US delegation was obliged to intervene and rewrite the South African proposal. In the final timetable, subsequently agreed, which ran up to November in Geneva, Brazzaville and New York, the Angolan–Cuban delegation reduced their original four-year withdrawal proposal to twenty-seven months.

The US delegation, led by Dr Chester Crocker, persistently, though inaccurately, briefed the Western press on the importance of the Soviet role in pressing the Cubans and the Angolans into compromise. The importance to Washington of this interpretation went well beyond the immediate negotiation and had an implication for US policy in South Africa itself, where considerable efforts were underway on many fronts to persuade the ANC to swing with the international climate of compromise and drop its armed struggle. However, no comparable new Western effort went into demanding that the South African government end the State of Emergency and release all political prisoners as a prelude to talks with the ANC. Dr Crocker's successful attempt to portray the Angolan situation as a replay of the settlement in Afghanistan, was useful in George Bush's presidential election campaign, as it reinforced the image of a Washington-mediated super-power relationship dominating regional conflicts.

There were, however, some parallels with the recent history of both Mozambique and Afghanistan. The ANC fighters' training camps, which had been one of the prides of independent Angola, gradually began to close towards the end of 1988, with the facilities to be reopened in Tanzania. For Pretoria to have thus squeezed the ANC military out of the Front-line States, with the exception of Tanzania, was an important goal to have achieved. In addition, the South Africans were able to rely on continuing US support for UNITA. This question was left out of the negotiations completely. Pretoria's own supplies to UNITA were supposed to stop after the final agreement was signed in New York in late December, but the Angolan military continued to report South African equipment being delivered well into 1989 – like the US-supported Mujahideen, UNITA was still well-equipped to fight on, despite the peace agreement. At the same time, and emphasizing the precariousness of Angola's agreement with South Africa, across the continent in Mozambique, South African logistical, training and supply support to the Mozambique National Resistance meant ambushes, sabotage and random killings continued as though the Nkomati Accord had never been signed nearly five years before.

But UNITA was useful to the South Africans in other ways, which went beyond mere destruction inside Angola. In the South African military camps of northern Namibia an unknown number of UNITA men were given identity cards which would allow them to vote in the UN-monitored elections that were to set the next phase of Namibia's history. No provisions were made in the complex quadripartite agreements for the future of the UNITA fighters based in South African military camps along the border. Ahead of any political arrangement which might take them back to Angola after more than ten years of fighting its government, preparations began to transform them into another destructive South African proxy force to destabilize an independent Namibia, as had been done to such devastating effect in Mozambique and Angola.

In flagrant disregard of the UN agreement, some men from Koevoet, the para-military unit long-used by the South Africans to terrorize civilians in northern Namibia, were integrated into the Namibian civilian police force. The Namibian armed forces, the South West Africa Territorial Force (SWATF) built up by the South Africans over the years to a 30,000-strong force, were nominally disbanded but in fact sent home on full pay until the end of September 1989. In mid-May a group of Koevoet, UNITA, and ex-SWAPO guerrillas turned traitors after capture by the South Africans, were sent into Angola wearing SWAPO uniforms. From the remote northern Namibian villages of Onheleiwa, Oshidobe, Enghoshi and Oikokola, villagers reported encampments of these men – modest grass-roof structures and defensive trenches. The scene was clearly set for continuing violent destabilization of Namibia through and after the independence process, with South Africa's client armed forces in an even stronger position after the early April massacres of SWAPO guerrillas.

The most significant precursors to that impending violence and the heaps of dead youths on 1 April, were the decisions made by the Security Council and the UN Secretary-General's office in New York in early 1989. These included the reduction in size of the UN monitoring force from the 7,500 men envisaged in 1978 to 4,650. The Non-Aligned Movement and the Organization of African Unity, led by the Front-line States, made repeated and fruitless appeals to the Security Council to revise the figure upwards. From the SWAPO leadership Secretary-General Toivo Ja Toivo even travelled to Moscow in an effort to persuade the Soviet Union not to accept the cut. But in the delicate stage of improving Soviet–US relations there was little chance that SWAPO's safety concerns would rate a Soviet confrontation with the US. These were early signs of the extent to which the two super-powers dominated the unfolding South West Africa peace process.

Another crucial change in the wording of the final UN documents also contributed to the débâcle of 1 April. The Secretary-General's final report spoke of the UN monitoring South African bases in Namibia, and SWAPO bases in Angola and Zambia. The issue of SWAPO's fighters already operating inside Namibia was simply ignored by the UN, intimidated by the fact that its processes under Resolution 435 were inextricably linked to what was decided between the US, South Africa, Cuba and Angola (with the Soviet Union as an observer) in the parallel negotiations. Pretoria's ever-present threat, within this group, to pull out of the whole jigsaw of arrangements became a routine way of undermining the UN. South Africa had, since 1979, always refused to admit that the 100,000-strong occupation force in Namibia was fighting an on-going guerrilla insurgency, though in the weeks before 1 April 1989 SADF military commanders in the north told journalists that SWAPO combatants were in the area doing political work among the population. Throughout March SWAPO leaders made repeated and unsuccessful efforts to get UN officials to discuss the issue of how and where these men would be confined to UN bases in the country. But South Africa had successfully intimidated the UN into shelving this problem as part of their effective marginalization of SWAPO.

This dangerous loose end was electric when coupled with the ambiguity of one of the secret agreements made between Angola, Cuba and South Africa. The Geneva Protocol of August 1988, on which Pretoria relied for justification for its 1 April attack on SWAPO, had provided for a withdrawal of troops to the north of the 16th Parallel 'within the context of the cessation of hostilities in Namibia'. With no ceasefire signed by South Africa as a prelude to UN Resolution 435, the clause was unclear – and deliberately so – allowing each party to interpret it as they wished. SWAPO had maintained some forces and heavy equipment in the border area on the Angolan side. They presumably anticipated that the guerrillas inside Namibia could face a serious security risk from the South

Africans even when confined to a base and monitored by a UN force, because this force was far too small to be an effective shield for them.

What no one could have forseen was that the UN, having first unleashed the South African military after the 1 April ceasefire, would then allow the South Africans to dictate that all SWAPO guerrillas must leave the country, back to Angola and north of the 16th Parallel. The South Africans' alternative offer that the guerrillas stay two days in a UN facility before going home unarmed was rejected out of hand by SWAPO as a recipe for assassinations. (No SWAPO supporter had forgotten the traumatic events which followed the 1978 false start to the UN process; SWAPO supporters who had demonstrated joyfully on the streets of Windhoek were photographed by the South Africans and became the objects of a systematic purge in which teachers, civil servants and many others lost their jobs, were reassigned to faraway posts, or separated from their families.) In May 1989 alone, more than 120 cases of harassment and violent intimidation against SWAPO supporters were reported by the United Nations in just the northern area of Oshakati. It was hardly a reassuring climate for the return of 50,000 or so refugee Namibians to their country. And the open canvassing by the South Africans for the various and shifting anti-SWAPO coalitions contesting the election, headed by the Democratic Turnhalle Alliance, increased the pressures and sense of foreboding that Pretoria had not relinquished the possibility of creating a client government for Namibia's future.

But such South African actions, as ever, barely seeped out to the wider world from Namibia's northern bush area. In June 1989 at the European Economic Commission in Brussels, Front-line States' Foreign Ministers lobbying for economic sanctions on South Africa to be extended to cover coal and agricultural products, found that the EEC mood had turned sharply away from exerting pressure on Pretoria. The progress towards independence in Namibia was held up as evidence of change in South Africa's policies. The EEC, led by Britain, called on the African Ministers not to rock the boat ahead of the South African elections in September 1989. More time was bought for the regime. The new leader of the National Party, Mr F. W. de Klerk, was received in London by Mrs Thatcher and in Bonn by Chancellor Helmut Kohl in a way that his predecessor, Mr P. W. Botha, had not been since 1984. The international community thus signalled that he was to be given the chance to show how different his policies would be from President Botha's. However, the talk of reform rang decidedly hollow against de Klerk's repeated commitment to ensuring white domination by a constitution which would enshrine 'group rights'.

Meanwhile, in Africa, the United States continued to put pressure on Angola to make the political deal with UNITA (possibly without Jonas Savimbi, at least initially) which US policy-makers had wanted for so long. From late 1988, with considerable US encouragement, a new regional grouping emerged, of Angola, Congo, Guinea, Gabon, Zambia, Zaïre and even Morocco, brought together for a number of meetings on Angola's future. The most dramatic meeting came in the Zaïrean town of Gbadolite in June 1989 when Angola's President Dos Santos met Jonas Savimbi and shook hands with him while announcing a ceasefire before seventeen African leaders. Within two months it had failed.

That meeting signalled the marginalizing of the Front-line States as a group, with their long tradition of practical and diplomatic solidarity for the liberation movements and their commitment to isolation of the South African regime. The military threat to all of them remained acute. The ANC itself had a 'red alert' in force in its offices throughout the region after a spate of poisonings and bomb attacks. Zimbabwe saw Pretoria escalate its threat, firstly by a series of attempted assassinations of ANC personnel by another group of Zimbabwean whites working for the South African military, and secondly by the stationing of its Cheetah fighter planes at Louis Trichard base near the Zimbabwe border. From there the planes could reach Dar Es Salaam, or ANC facilities in Tanzania, without refuelling. Vulnerable Botswana also found itself under renewed pressure.

It was a signal of the changing times that Zaïre's Foreign Minister Nguza Karl i Bond (once Zaïre's best known dissident, who had been the one to tell a US Congressional Committee in 1981 that President Mobutu and his family were transferring $60 million a year from the Bank of Zaïre to their overseas accounts) now emerged as the pivot in a new round of shuttle diplomacy moving further towards ending South Africa's isolation. Zaïre, so long the US's key conduit for military support for Savimbi, was the obvious candidate to lead the next phase of US regional policy beyond political change in Angola to the return of South Africa to normal status in the international community, and towards the end of the threat of economic sanctions. Not only did Karl i Bond visit South Africa, but even the Soviet Deputy Foreign Minister, Anatoly Adamishin paid a visit (kept secret for some months) and Zambia's President Kenneth Kaunda broke the Front-line States' common position of a decade (always excepting Mozambique) and met Mr de Klerk.

The breaking down of the policy of isolating South Africa was nowhere more evident than in the military field. By mid-1989 South Africa was preparing the first test of a medium-range ballistic missile, manufactured, despite the UN arms embargo of 1977, with Israeli aid. Its 900-mile range menaced all the Front-line States directly. In 1988 and 1989 Chile and Turkey both defied the UN and hosted South Africa at international arms exhibitions, while European governments such as Finland and Holland ordered South Africa's Crotale missile system.

But such normalization of Pretoria's world role was in stark contrast to the mood of the black majority inside the country who began a systematic breaking of restrictions, banning orders and other rules of the State of Emergency. At the same time there was an unprecedented flow of political groups, businessmen, academics and churchmen to Lusaka to consult with the ANC. Oliver Tambo for the ANC, and every leader of the black community, reiterated the same call for ending the State of Emergency, freeing all political prisoners, lifting the ban on all political organizations as the preliminary moves to negotiations on a new constitution. But one man, one vote, in the unitary state of South Africa was still far from Mr de Klerk's plans.

Epilogue

Resistance: children of the townships

When the first bus-load of passengers off the flight from
Johannesburg walked through the glass doors into the Harare
Sheraton hotel and saw Oliver Tambo, President of the
long-banned African National Congress, gasps of astonishment turned quickly to singing of freedom songs which echoed
through the lobby. 'Marching to Pretoria' was taken up by
dozens of voices and emphasized by the characteristic
rhythmic thud of South African dancing. Dozens of arms
grasped the small dark-suited figure of Oliver Tambo and
raised him shoulder high. As though they had known him for
years they hugged him, kissed him, called him 'Sir', 'Mr
President' or 'Comrade'. Once, as a lawyer, long ago, he had
been a young township activist like so many of them, beaver-
ing away at any loophole in the apartheid laws which con-
strained every aspect of their lives. Old women with drawn
faces, in the knitted hats and bright nylon dresses of all of
urban Africa, and young elegant women with elaborate
plaited hair and swinging earrings, cried openly with the shock
of meeting this man. Next to the imprisoned Nelson Mandela,
he has for all the years of his exile loomed largest in the myths
and ideology which have shaped South Africa's people's
resistance to the white regime.

The Harare conference on children, repression and torture
in South Africa, held in September 1987, was the background
to these momentous meetings. The conference was organized
with great difficulty, and had suffered one five-month post-
ponement, partly because some argued that the risks of South
African terrorist attacks against the participants or Zimbabwean targets were too great. South African readiness to hit
ANC targets in the centre of Harare had been demonstrated

too frequently, and too recently, for such a risk to be discounted. Others argued that the risks mattered little against a chance of lifting another of Brecht's blankets of silence – this one on the apartheid regime's systematic terrorizing, torture and psychological stunting of South Africa's children.

The responsibility of convener lay with the lifelong campaigner against apartheid, the British Bishop, Trevor Huddleston, once an Anglican priest in the South African township of Sophiatown, but squeezed out by Pretoria. Seeing him beaming in the jostling crowd it was easy to forget that he was almost seventy and in poor health. Participants from inside the country were chosen mostly by the Church, and from outside largely by the external wing of the ANC. The host was the Law Faculty of the University of Zimbabwe.

Those four days in the Zimbabwean capital were a watershed in both South African and regional politics. Myths died, barriers broke, before the realities of face-to-face contacts. Courage and endurance were reinforced for the many-faceted battles to maintain resistance and strengthen morale, which most people in that hall were engaged in. The meeting gave a foretaste of the strengths and talents of a South African post-apartheid society, though none there had any illusion that such a thing was within easy reach.

For many of those who came from within South Africa it was their first trip outside the country. The apartheid government, by censorship, by the Bantu education act ('education for servitude' as Prime Minister Verwoerd had called it), and by mass detentions of leaders, has tried to enforce not only the physical controls of apartheid but control too over its citizens' minds.

The extent of Pretoria's failure in imposing that control was underscored for everyone who came from outside, including the ANC exiled leadership. Those first fiery moments of excited meetings set the tone between people who often knew remarkably little about each other as individuals. But their political lives depended largely on their trust for each other, built up by a network of internal organization, high-risk meetings and messages through go-betweens, the ANC's broadcasts on its station Radio Freedom, and the then still unbanned UDF's carefully judged escalation of its opposition to Pretoria.

From those first minutes in Harare not only the leadership of the ANC, but also the Front-line States and particularly the host Zimbabwe, could gauge at first hand one thing: how remote to these little-known fighters was any possibility of compromise or peace negotiations with the Goliath of power in Pretoria, or indeed its couriers from the boardrooms or government offices of London or Washington. The devastation wrought by South Africa on the Front-line States, relatively well known compared with what South African censorship had hidden under its state of emergency, appeared in a clearer war context. The South African children and mothers who spoke so openly in Harare, over the border from the censor, for the townships' front line, called for peace – on their terms. Those terms were dictated by the level of popular resistance they had organized, and the depth of suffering and sacrifice which it meant. To them, one person one vote in a unitary state which saw the end of the apartheid regime and its Bantustans was not a negotiating position but an achievable goal.

About 300 South Africans had travelled to Harare, two thirds of them from inside the country and about sixty from the exiled ANC. Few of the priests, doctors, lawyers, social workers, journalists and community organizers from inside who had come with statistics, affidavits and in some cases the actual child victims of torture and their mothers, knew that the ANC leaders would be at Harare. They had come to try to reach the world, not the ANC leadership.

Fewer still knew that Oliver Tambo himself and almost half the 30-strong ANC National Executive Committee would come. 'If I had known I would have been even more terrified, but even more keen to attend,' said one young lawyer. 'The South Africans no doubt knew. They might decide to wipe us all out here, or pick us up one by one when we get back. But it no longer matters, new layers of leadership emerge with every mass detention.' It was the sentiment echoed by delegates as different as the well-heeled white women of the liberal Black Sash organization to the tough young comrades of the townships. The yawning gap of a lifetime's experience between the comfortable, still safe suburbia which lay behind the former, and the underground life of total personal sacrifice of the latter was easily bridged, not only in the shared concern for the children at the centre of the conference, but in the impact on them of normal life outside the reach of apartheid's deformations.

The smallest of everyday exchanges struck some of them as forcibly as the late-night, carefully structured meetings preparing for a common future, which formed a backdrop to the days of formal meetings on children. In a lift in the Sheraton with a uniformed Zimbabwean policeman one of the young men from South Africa stared at his face, then said 'How are you, man?' After the policeman went out with a brief greeting, the South African said, gazing after him with astonishment, 'These people have got their independence, I can talk to a policeman, I could probably ride in his car. How far away is something like that at home – I couldn't even have imagined it.' Similarly stunned, a young white doctor who found his allocated roommate, also a doctor, was not only black but from the external mission of the ANC, said 'This is absolutely amazing, I can't work out how these things could happen.'

In the great ballroom of the Sheraton the coincidences, or not, of the dining arrangements, put Joe Slovo, General-Secretary of the long outlawed South African Communist Party and former Chief of Staff of the ANC's armed wing Umkhonto we Sizwe, next to the scion and moral scourge of the conservative Afrikaner Church, Reverend Beyers Naude, former Secretary-General of the South African Council of Churches (SACC). 'When I was first approached about this meeting on children I said only a miracle could let us bring perhaps fifty or sixty people to it from South Africa. In fact we could have added 400 or so more names who wanted to come. This has started something no action of the state, however repressive, can stop,' said Naude speaking for his constituency at home.

In his introduction for after-dinner speaker, Reverend Frank Chikane, Naude's successor as SACC Secretary General, Thabo Mbeki, the ANC's publicity secretary paid tribute to the Church's grand old men who for most of their adult lives had headed the moral crusade against apartheid: Beyers Naude and Bishop Trevor Huddleston.

'We are the true patriots, we stand for truth. True patriotism, true loyalty to our country is trying to say to the world, "Liberate us from this tyranny, the government is leading us to national suicide",' the Reverend Naude said. He closed his speech on a sombre note, voicing the preoccupation ebbing and flowing in many conversations that day. 'It adds to my anguish that dozens of us here who don't, like me, have the protection of being well-known, have still got to go back. I hope that nothing will happen, I pray that nothing will happen. But those who do pay a price will pay it for all of us.' Everyone knew the price he meant was detention, torture, or even death.

There was a long standing ovation that night for the two elderly churchmen (Naude and Huddleston), born outsiders to these communities, but long since become integral parts of them. The next day's closing speech of the working session was from a young Muslim Sheik who symbolized the opposition's transition from a moral crusade to civil war. Faried Esack, of The Call of Islam, an affiliate organization of the UDF, started his speech with the name of Allah, then spelt out to the two Christian priests and to Oliver Tambo, 'President of our national liberation movement', what many had said informally to these men they had chosen as their unchallenged leaders. 'Thank you for preventing our struggle from degenerating into a black versus white confrontation; thank you for standing with us for truth versus falsehood; thank you for standing with us for justice versus injustice.'

Faried Esack and the Anglican churchman Frank Chikane represent the same generation of remarkably young leaders which emerged at the head of the South African Resistance in the mid-1980s. Since the late 1960s the mass repression, the life sentences in prison, the eliminating of individuals by death, exile, banning orders, refusal of passports, blackmail and intimidation into treachery, pushed resistance deep underground, so that, looking across the crowded hall, it appeared a middle generation was missing. The older generation who had survived inside the country were, apart from Beyers Naude, and the mothers of some of the ANC guerrillas executed by Pretoria, conspicuously absent in this gathering.

Reverend Frank Chikane, half the age of his predecessor though just as confident, took the edge off many people's anxieties by a levity startling to an outsider, but characteristic of many South Africans these days. He said, 'People wonder why we are always laughing in the face of detentions, deaths, so much violence. That mixture of joy and pain, laughter and tears, is our strength.' He raised roars of laughter when he started his speech by musing on how he could address Oliver Tambo 'without becoming part of another treason trial'. He went on, 'If I call him "Honorable President" this is a crime. This is subversive. No one must speak positively of the ANC.'

The laughs echoed on appreciatively at other tables where Pretoria's rules were being broken with joy as the ANC delegates were sprinkled among other delegates. A former Robben Island prisoner, now in exile, asked avidly for news of streets, districts, landmarks long since transformed by the tricks of memory. Everywhere were the confident faces of the 1976 generation of teenagers who fled the country after the police massacre of Soweto schoolchildren. Now, after working for ten years with the ANC, they were again meeting old friends or relations from a different phase of their lives.

The absurd side of Pretoria's ban on the ANC had never been more evident than in that Sheraton ballroom. Thabo Mbeki, for instance, sat with a lawyer cousin from home whom he had not seen for fourteen years, while Ruth Mompati, once ANC representative in London and now a National Executive Committee member, sat among a group of women from the townships who had lost guerrilla sons, or had husbands detained on Robben Island for life. One mother of four detained children, who had even brought her eleven-year-old son to testify in Harare, arrived late and harassed-looking at dinner. Within seconds Ruth Mompati stood up to give her her seat.

The impact of such a small personal gesture, like Joe Slovo's patient listening to a young man (who said later he had wanted to discuss whether 'the ANC could be as committed to the rights of gays as to the rights of women') stunned the South African group from inside the country as much as anything else. 'They are all so human, and we've got so used to expecting only inhumanity from anyone with power,' said a delegate. One doctor, reeling away from a handshake with Oliver Tambo said, 'He thanked *me* for *my* work and said it was a privilege to meet me, before I could get the words out to say, "it's quite the other way round, Mr President".' The South African government was then running an advertising campaign, especially in Commonwealth countries ahead of the Vancouver Commonwealth summit, which portrayed the 'gruesome murderers of the ANC, led by Oliver Tambo and Joe Slovo.' The words could hardly have struck a more unconvincing and counterproductive note.

Mrs Thatcher two weeks later pulled the veil off the British government's real feelings about the ANC by saying at Vancouver that the ANC was 'a terrorist organization'. She could not more clearly have shown her fear of listening to the future South Africa, and her blind conviction that force would decide the future. After Vancouver, where she stood, again, alone against economic sanctions she was hailed by white South Africa as an honorary citizen. It was hardly an accolade that anyone with a sense of history, or of human dignity, would have wanted.

As Bishop Trevor Huddleston said in Harare, 'The thing that sickens me from all these Western politicians I have been talking to all these years is the appalling assumption that it doesn't matter if it takes five, ten, fifteen, twenty years to end apartheid, and meanwhile hundreds of thousands of children are destroyed.'

Listening to children, some not even in their teens, speak of being beaten for hours, kicked by five or six soldiers, taken from their homes during the night, kept in local police stations or John Vorster Square's notorious interrogation rooms, in solitary confinement, put in a car boot, in a fridge, in a rubber suit to which electrodes were attached, made to stare at bright lights, to stand for twelve-hour periods, shackled wrist to ankle, forced to listen to other children screaming, was the stuff of nightmares. (In a revealing use of the classic Western press tradition of deadening real political drama in order to be able to puff up convenient apolitical ones, the *Washington Post* chose to describe these testimonies as 'a tactic in the battle with South Africa for world opinion' and 'a key weapon in the ANC's public relations arsenal'.)

Even though he had, as he said, heard it all before, Frank Chikane left the room in pain during the children's testimony. He was not alone. The tears of adults, however, seemed inappropriate before these children who see themselves as guerrillas, with a legitimate right and duty to fight back against the state which is shattering their future. They, like the Princeton Law Professor Richard Falk, pointed the conference towards the concept that this South African state terrorism, torture, fracturing individuals, families and communities, was as deliberate and systematic a political act as Hitler's Germany's crushing of Jews, gypsies and communists. As Faried Esack said, 'There was law and order in Germany, but at what cost to humankind?'

The nationalism that motivates these children is a variant of the kind of Third-World nationalism which has long been seen as a threat by successive US administrations, and is always deformed and scorned by the cynics in the Western media. Guatemala under Arbenz, Cambodia under Sihanouk, Chile under Allende, Ghana under Nkrumah, Congo under Lumumba, Greece between 1965 and 1967, Grenada under Bishop, Burkina under Sankara – all are examples of regimes which sought to build modest political, economic and cultural independence from the West, as Southern Africa is doing today, and South Africa's children will do tomorrow. In most of these cases the United States, with the knowledge of other Western powers, employed covert means to change the course of their history, as was later testified by those involved at the time.

One of the victims, Sihanouk, put it like this to the Greek Andreas Papandreou, then in exile after the Colonels' coup: 'The only thing I had not anticipated was that the United States would take part directly in trying to take our country to pieces . . . we were being punished, humiliated, and prepared for the chopping block because we had stood on our dignity. We refused to become US puppets or join the anti-communist crusade. We spurned the billion-dollar rewards for such a role. That was our crime in the eyes of successive US administrations.' Papandreou's response at the time was, 'These phrases could easily have been written by a Greek.' Similar ones have been, by many Africans.

In the exiled ANC and the now banned UDF the United States has again come up against the powerful force of a nationalism it does not care to understand. But yesterday's easy destructive victories of imperialism over hidden lives far from the metropolis will not be repeated in South Africa. Never, except in the Vietnamese war against the US, has there been a comparable level of popular organization and a readiness for personal sacrifice for freedom, involving a whole population from its old women to its young children.

After Harare's unprecedented opportunity to consult with those on the front-line inside South Africa there was a long meeting of the ANC's National Executive Committee. From this, it was no coincidence that an historic statement on the state of the civil war emerged. In its 9 October 1987 statement the ANC again repeated its refusal of the many secret negotiations half-offered by Pretoria, and rejected outright President Botha's proposed National Statutory Council. The leaders refused all demands to end the armed struggle and attempts to split the ANC from the South African Communist Party. Their conditions for negotiation remained constant: unconditional release of all political prisoners, cessation of all political trials, lifting of the state of emergency, police to be withdrawn from the townships and confined to their barracks, repeal of all repressive legislation, a fixed time-frame for negotiations. The clarity was a kind of homage from the leaders in exile to the courage and endurance revealed at Harare by so many unknown individuals – children, mothers, priests, doctors.

'Children who should be playing hide-and-seek are hiding for their lives from police,' said Reverend Chikane; 'we don't know where to hide these children, our Ministry is almost underground.' Another young priest, from the Detainees' Parents Support Committee said, 'Children view liberation as more important than their own lives.' Such feelings were commonly expressed by several of the children who came to Harare to testify publicly on their own experiences of torture and detention that had made them flee the country. One, now at the ANC's school in Tanzania said, 'I'm studying now, but later I will go back to South Africa and fight against apartheid.' These are composed youths, honed not only by the terrible experiences forced on them by South African police torturers, but by the responsibilities they took on themselves in their local youth organizations or school councils. During the township upheavals of the early 1980s several of them were marshals organizing peaceful marches at funerals or rent boycotts or were leaders of struggles within their schools for a new curriculum that would not be bound by Vorster's 'Bantu education' concept, or for the removal of police from the campus. They related such things as learning to live underground, sleeping away from home for months 'for safety' and then being betrayed to police by one of their very own group, or being pointed out to police by a school mate who had been one of the most articulate in calling for school boycotts, demonstrations, or building barricades against the police and soldiers. Informers, *agents provocateurs*, blackmail, are not the stuff of war stories or spy novels to these children. They have learned to survive abrupt withdrawals of trust with a steely maturity not granted to people who grow up in more normal circumstances.

Like the children of Namibia, of Angola, of Mozambique, and other African countries, in those Cuban schools so far away, these unknown children of the townships have the inspiring confidence in a different future which is the gift of those who choose to be fighters. The heroes of the other African countries and of other generations like Agostinho Neto, Lucio Lara, Murtala Mohamed, Houari Boumedienne, Mustafa El Ouali, and Thomas Sankara would recognize these children – heirs of a tradition of resistance.

Index

Organizations have been indexed under their acronyms, e.g. ANC, IMF, SWAPO. For a full list of acronyms and abbreviations, see page xv.